Beyond the Killing Tree

A JOURNEY OF DISCOVERY

STEPHEN REYNOLDS

EPICENTER PRESS

FAIRBANKS/SEATTLE

92 h
Reynolds

Editor: Don Graydon
Dust jacket/book design/typesetting: Elizabeth Watson
Proofreader: Christine Ummel
Dust jacket/text illustrations: Gail Niebrugge
Maps: Gail Niebrugge
Production: Ripinsky & Co.

A portion of Chapter 9 and parts of Chapters 4 and 8 appeared previously in an article published in *New Mexico Wildlife* magazine. A portion of Chapter 3 appeared in an article published in *Northwest Parks and Wildlife* magazine.

Library of Congress Cataloging-in-Publication Data
    Reynolds, Stephen, 1937 Nov. 23-
    Beyond the killing tree : a journey of discovery / Stephen Reynolds.
       p.   cm.
    ISBN 0-945397-42-9
    1. Reynolds, Stephen, 1937 Nov. 23-   2. Game wardens—Alaska—Biography. 3. Game wardens—New Mexico—Biography. 4. Hunting—Moral and ethical aspects. I. Title.
    SK367.R49   1995
    639.9'092—dc20
    [B]   95-22083
                                                              CIP

To order single, autographed copies of *Beyond the Killing Tree*, send $19.95 (Washington residents add $1.64 for state sales tax) plus $5 for priority-mail shipping to: Epicenter Press, Box 82368, Kenmore, WA 98028. Booksellers: Retail discounts are available from our trade distributor, Graphic Arts Center Publishing Co., Portland, Oregon, at 800-452-3032.

Printed in the United States of America

10 9 8 7 6 5 4 3 2 1

For

JUDY MARIE

Hot coffee at forty below—cold hands and a warm heart!

and

For

ELOISE R. R. REAM

Keep looking for the white-horse days.

CONTENTS

Preface

This book is from the heart. No apologies.

Not so long ago I was an avid hunter, and for a time I trapped predatory animals in the name of "wildlife protection." I also spent a few years as a guide and professional hunter. But for most of my life, I was a game warden, working as an officer in wildlife conservation. Actually, I should specify game animal and livestock conservation because that was what our fish and game agencies were dedicated to, and still are for the most part: protecting wild and domestic meat animals from other life-forms for the primary benefit of the sport hunter and the rancher. We've been like Farmer Brown guarding his barnyard from the fox—except the barnyard in this case happens to be the wildlife habitats of our nation.

As a young man I did not understand the sensitivity that welled within me for wildlife, which I was taught to take not only for food, but simply to take: to kill for the sport of killing, a diversion beyond need. It was thought a weakness to feel a consideration for other life-forms. I overcame that so-called weakness and soon learned to kill with the rest of the hunting fraternity, justifying the killing as a primal heritage or, in the case of predators, for the good of game and domestic animal conservation.

I spent most of my life working in backcountry areas, and my loyalties regarding the uses of wild things began to reverse over time. I found myself at odds with previous convictions. Is it possible for the opposing selves of exploitation and preservation within each of us to come to terms?

The stories in this book follow my experiences of transition as I faced up to this question. The transition came not only from within, but also from changes that surrounded me during a series of

6

adventures across half a century of living and working in two totally different parts of the country, the high desert and mountains of the Southwest and the vast and varied terrain of Alaska. Some of the happenings are humorous, some are not. But all are stories of outdoors adventures and of the passages we make as we learn different concepts and exchange old ideas for new.

An old supervisor of mine asked me one day what the condition of the Rio Grande was when I had driven across it that morning. Was it running high or low, muddy or clear? Were there any fishermen in sight of the bridge, and if so, were they catching any fish? And if they were, what were they using for bait? Did they all have their licenses? I told him I didn't know the answer to any of those questions, because I hadn't even looked off the bridge as I went by. He never said another word, and neither did I. We both knew a good game warden would know the answer to those questions. I never went across a bridge after that without looking over the conditions; but he never asked me the question again, though I worked with him for several years. He knew I would always have the answer.

While writing this book, there were times I felt that old supervisor's presence, looking over my shoulder, ready to ask me about a particular observation. But I was ready for him—ready to answer for anything I said, ready to admit if I didn't know the answer. So I hope you won't find many times that I fail to make a fair and careful observation within these pages, but if you do, please forgive me the way he once did.

I want to welcome you to these scenes and experiences of the open country, of time spent with people, the land, and animals, all in some phase of transition. I hope the stories touch a part of your own spirit of change.

Acknowledgments

I began this book almost twenty years ago with a story of a mountain lion in a tree. I asked Jim Rearden, at that time a writer and editor with *Alaska Magazine*, to review it as a favor. I now wish to thank Jim for the thoughtful comments, suggestions, and encouragement that carried me, eventually, into other facets of the manuscript.

Something should be said of the various sporting magazines that rejected that first story, due partly to its sensitivity toward the quarry and its incompatibility with what they thought their readers wanted. Those rejections gave me cause to realize I had something to contribute—another side to issues of hunting for sport. I thank these magazines for helping to set me on the correct course.

I wish to thank my wife, Judy, for not only condoning this writing habit of mine, but for giving me honest and valuable criticism and assistance as the manuscript took form. I thank Kent Sturgis for opening the door to publication and Don Graydon for his soft style of hard editing. And thank you, Feral Macloud—your enthusiasm for the written word was inspiring.

The following people, some long gone, have unknowingly contributed to this book by providing lasting impressions and images for a young wildlife officer: M. F. Embrey, Nando Mauldin, Bill Humphries, Shelvy Lowrance, Tom Rogers, Roy Owen, George and Verna Hightower, Shorty Lyon, Bear Turner, Roy Snyder, Hugh Olney, Walter and Ruby Rodgers, Charley Bird, Jim McClellan, Carl Berghofer, Louis Berghofer, R. W. Raught, Elliot S. Barker, Bill Huey, John Shaul, Frank Smith, T. J. Ramsey, Alton Ford, and Dick Brown.

*"It is in the land . . . that one searches
out and eventually finds what is beautiful.
And an edge of this deep and rarefied beauty
is the acceptance of complex paradox and
the forgiveness of others."*

—Barry Lopez
Arctic Dreams

> *"We should come home from far,*
> *from adventures, and perils,*
> *and discoveries every day,*
> *with new experience and character."*

—Henry David Thoreau
A Week on the Concord and Merrimack Rivers

PART ONE

DISCOVERY

It's as though our genes—our souls—understand why we feel a comfort out under a bush in the rain, even if our minds do not.

CHAPTER ONE

Kid on the Loose

Hunters were the role models of my youth: my father, my uncles, my brother-in-law. Their limited free time was saturated with hunting and fishing. I still hear echoes of their voices, turning adventures into yarns, repeated and repeated but always exciting to me. I see myself in my bedroom, straining to hear the tales through the late-night wall into the living room; laughter about kicking the coffee pot into the fire; silence as a deep voice describes a stalk, while someone imitates the chirping call of a wild turkey hen.

It was in their genes, the need to hunt and wander. It is in the genes of all men, I believe, diluted almost to nonexistence in our urban culture. For myself, though, there is something beyond an urge to hunt, kill, return with the spoils: there is a connectedness with the woods and mountains, the open expanses of the desert, the sea—the living energy of it all. It's as though our genes—our souls—understand why we feel a comfort out under a bush in the rain, even if our minds do not.

I don't recall the men of my family talking about the beauty of a particular scene or demonstrating a respect for the animals they hunted and killed. Perhaps the evolution down through generations had failed to bring with it the respect once practiced by my Cherokee ancestors in giving thanks to the animal presenting itself, or the ritual carried out by my European forefathers in placing a green twig, signifying a last meal, in the mouth of the animal taken, all of which may mean something, or nothing whatsoever, depending on who you are; however, a ritual may have taught me early on to pause for contemplation—taught me to take some time to consider the meanings of life for some and death for others, and an appreciation for the sacrifice of one life to replenish the life of another.

AS A KID, I WANDER AROUND like a loose dog, all over town, then all over the countryside, capturing blue-tailed lizards, horned toads, crawdads, soft-shell turtles, and English sparrows (if a horned toad grabs you, he won't turn loose till lightning strikes). There's a kid who works down on the railroad docks unloading watermelons; he rolls one off for the rest of us now and then. *Splat.* Rusty corrugated-tin shed roofs in that part of town, hot to climb on unshod; sit on the hot tin and pee down the grooves. Did you ever watch someone defecate from high in a cottonwood tree? Interesting, but do not stand directly under. All in the life of a nomadic urchin.

As a young hunter of twelve or so, I hitch a ride with my mother out to the desert mesa east of Albuquerque, where she drops me off to hunt coyotes. The hunt mainly involves examining and tormenting stink bugs, stirring up red ants, and taking potshots with my .22 Winchester single-shot at long-range jackrabbits (or things that could be). The only coyote I ever see is at a distance, loping far away at a leisurely pace across the sparse gramma grass and tumbleweeds, grinning back at me, with long ears standing erect and tongue trailing in the wind, watching me constantly, not where he is going it seems to me, and hypnotizing me to where I forget I am supposed to shoot. His presence gives me the satisfaction of knowing I am in a truly wild country, and of course, that is where I long to be.

I look into the darkness of a rabbit hole—I look into all the holes, daring the rabbits to show themselves—and see the large brown eye of a jackrabbit peering back at me out of the blackness of a cool shadow. It is a methodical eye; wild, but without fear—staring as though it could see inside of me. I recoil and shamefully realize I'm not the tough hunter I thought. I won't tell my old man about it, only about the coyote, and that I wasn't close enough for a killing shot.

By the time I'm thirteen my father decides I'm old enough to go deer hunting with him and his friends. The friends don't take too kindly to the idea; but then, they are not the sort of friends who take their sons hunting. Their idea of a hunting trip is a bottle of booze and a deck of cards, although I know my old man was not that sort. These are one-day hunts. Leave at two in the morning; arrive in the hills at daybreak; friends stumble out of the car and sight-in rifles by firing at rocks on the hillside, scattering any deer within three miles; walk the hills all day, then try to figure out where they are from the car about thirty minutes before dark; search for each other and honk the horn half the night trying to lead the lost ones back.

But although the old man loved to hunt, he never owned a rifle, always borrowed one; never thought he could afford a high-powered rifle. But he let me use the only firearm he ever owned—his twelve-gauge Remington pump shotgun loaded with slugs—while he carried someone else's rifle. We never bagged a deer then, nor do I recall that he ever talked of having killed one. He was a small-game hunter, though he wouldn't hunt doves, said they were the bird of peace, and wouldn't hunt rabbits in any month not having an "R" in it, the summer months being the time for fleas. The nearest we came to bagging anything other than rabbits, squirrels, or quail was a turkey. Dad was asleep under a pine tree and I watched a flock of turkeys feed their way right up to us, then feed their way away from us. I was fascinated by their activity and never made a move, so mesmerized by it all that I forgot to wake the old man. He was plenty mad because they had gotten away. He didn't think it was funny, even later.

MY DAD WAS A HARD MAN to know. Maybe it came from being "the man of the house" since he was eleven, when his father died. I think he must have felt the weight of that responsibility all his life.

His father, Bob, died during the Spanish flu epidemic of 1919. My dad's mother, Minnie, was twenty-six then—twenty-six years old, with five little kids. Dad was the oldest at age eleven. His father had been working in the oil fields at Burkburnette, Texas. He said the last time he saw him, he came out to the pasture and said he was going away to work for a while, and that Dad would have to be the man of the house now.

They were living over on Sugar Creek, near Gotebo, Oklahoma, getting by on a few staples and on small game Dad would bag with his little .22 single-shot rifle. One day, when the creek was swollen with rainwater, his Uncle Ray and Aunt Frances called to them from across the high water; shouted across that Bob was sick with the flu and needed Minnie in Burkburnette. Uncle Ray tied some money in a sock and threw it across the creek, and Aunt Frances tossed over her shoes for Minnie to wear when she caught the train to Texas.

At Burkburnette she nursed him, but he died anyway, the man of her life. I remember an earlier picture of her with him; she was young and pretty, the light of a new happiness in her bright eyes. She took the thousand dollars insurance money and spent it all on a large marble tombstone; and them living on beans and corn bread; living on a dirt floor in a dugout near Gotebo.

Years later, my grandmother remarried. His name was Hiram Gill, and he was a heavy-bellied western fellow with a great red, swollen face—round, like a smiling moon. He was always cheerful with me, and had a big, slobbering bulldog who would charge across the room and grab my leg, pulling me out of the chair, whenever Hi told him to. "Bo, go git ol' Steve's pant leg!" Bo would growl and slobber and tear at my trousers as if he meant to smother or drown whatever it was the pants represented. I didn't know whether to be scared or not, and must have had big eyes, because everyone would laugh, and so would I after a while, in a way. Then later, when I was older, I saw a picture of Bo, and he was just a little Boston bull.

Someone said Hi was an alcoholic, and I heard later he

was killed in a head-on collision while crossing a narrow bridge north of Socorro, New Mexico. Drunk, they said. He's buried there next to my grandmother, Minnie, in the gray sand and dry tumbleweeds west of Socorro. My dad took me there once when I was a kid, while Hi was still alive. It was after World War II; Minnie had died while Dad was gone for two years to the Aleutian Islands. We stopped on the plaza in Socorro to see Hi Gill before we went out to search through the greasewood and mesquite. Hi didn't go with us.

I wonder what it would be like to be left the man of the house at eleven years of age. I don't think I really knew my dad or what he had gone through in life. Maybe I understand him better now that I am older—now that he is gone, his ashes scattered in the Valle Grande of New Mexico; his father buried beneath a grass lawn and big tombstone in Duncan, Oklahoma, and his mother in the desert weeds west of Socorro, next to old Hi Gill.

*I look out the window from the
third floor. The snow must be in the
hills by now; the track of a coyote
seems like a free thought.*

CHAPTER TWO

Renegade

It is 1954, and I sit looking out my window in "C" Company
barracks on the third floor, where the new cadets, the "rats,"
live. I look out toward the free fields beyond the manicured
lawns and heavy shade trees, and I wonder what could have
possessed me to impose such a sentence on myself. I think,
Christ, now you've done it.

Used to be kids were sent away to military schools.
Ornery kids, renegades. But not all; some were from military
families, sent by tradition. Many were from wealthy families,
sent again by tradition. I'm not sure any longer why I went,
other than that I was a bit of a renegade. But I wasn't sent to
military school, I asked to go. Maybe I realized I would never
make it through high school without the club of discipline
over my head. I had already left public high school partway
through my junior year, deciding I would rather spend the
days hiking the mountains and exploring the caves east of
Albuquerque. My father said, "You don't want to go to
school? Then go to work." And I began to pay rent. After
half a year of that, I realized I could never get a job as a forest
ranger or a game warden without at least a high school

education, so I asked to go to military school. Christ!

The ocher brick barracks at New Mexico Military Institute, filled with what seem like prison cells, face inward toward an open courtyard. There's a nice view from the third floor. And from here you can quickly get down to the lower floors when an old cadet shouts for you. All upperclassmen are old cadets, and there are six classes of them, all the way to college seniors. But the seniors are not demanding; over the years, they have grown tired of the power of hazing. It's the young old cadets who are the dangerous ones. We rats do not walk anywhere, we run. And when we stop, we stand at attention, and we say "sir" to all old cadets: "Sir, reporting as you requested, sir."

"Well, butthead, since three other rats outran you down here, then you get the job of shining these boots." I take the boots and head upstairs on the run. "RAT!" Another old cadet spots me, and there are more boots to shine. The trick is somehow staying out of sight up on the third floor, but you cannot stay there forever. Once you're down on the lower floors, it's hard to make it back without being hailed by every old cadet who sees you.

I once purposely take back mismatched boots—size nine left, size ten right. The two old cadets hobble out late to formation after struggling into uncomfortable boots at the last minute. I pay for it with an ass beating. There are three kinds of ass beatings from which you may select: coat hanger, toothbrush, or broom. You better take the broom. The toothbrush is the worst: Bend over, grab your ankles, bare ass; toothbrush held flat against the hide, bent back and snapped. It will raise a half-inch welt. And the coat hanger uncoiled and used as a whip is criminal.

Discovery

Physical hazing is forbidden by the Institute's rules of conduct, but that particular rule is winked at. Not so the rule against drinking, or the rule against stealing, or the ones against lying or cheating. It's an early introduction to the rule that some rules are not rules. The question is, which rules can you break without getting broken yourself? Something more defined than any rule, though, is the unwritten code that you never officially complain. It would not occur to anyone to blow the whistle on another cadet or the system.

This is an honor school. You will be expelled for many things. I don't do those things, but I do every other questionable thing and don't miss by much the maximum number of tours and demerits allowed. A tour is an hour of walking uniformed, M-1 rifle in prescribed military fashion, to and fro and around and across the quadrangle. I do hundreds of tours. Nights, weekends, holidays. Can you tour the renegade out of someone?

"Flatheads" they call us in town, because of the shape of our dress hats. We are allowed to leave the Institute grounds only for a few hours on Saturday and Sunday afternoons. The public high school boys in Roswell hate the sight of us. We walk down the sidewalks on Saturday and they drive by: "FLATHEADS!" We "date" their girlfriends; take them to the Friday hop. The girls have to get their own ride to the Institute, meet us there, walk fifty yards over to the ballroom, then get their own ride back home. We are not allowed cars. I may have had one date in two years. I cannot see the point in it. In the mind of a teenage boy, what is there to do if there's no back seat?

At the Institute we memorize inanities to be instantly upchucked whenever asked. Sometimes we don't know the answer, but there is an answer even for that: "Sir, not having been informed to the fullest degree of accuracy, I hesitate to articulate for the fear of deviating from the correct path of rectitude."

"How is a cow?"
"Sir, she walks, she talks, she's full of chalk; the lacteal fluid extracted from the female of the bovine species is highly prolific to the Nth degree."

But this is a serious institution here. This is the place where leadership is born, they say. Later, when you are out in the real world of business and politics and battle-planning, you will join the Rotary Club, dress smartly—nothing less than a Windsor knot in that tie, please—and be on your way to a life of conformity, maintaining an image of utmost respectability.

March to chow, march to the laundry, march to PE; and then to drill practice, where we march some more. Inspections each morning, formal review and marching in parade on weekends. But I don't mind the marching; it is the only time we do not have to run.

September, October, November, December . . .

I look out the window from the third floor. The snow must be in the hills by now; high in the mountains it lies deep; the track of a coyote seems like a free thought. I wonder what it would be like to drive along the highway and see weeds growing.

"How do you make leather?"
"Sir, if the fresh skin of an animal is cleaned and divested of all

*hair, fat, and extraneous matter, and immersed into a diluted
solution of tannic acid, a chemical combination ensues; the gelatinous
tissue of the skin is transformed into a nonproteolysable substance,
impervious to, and insoluble in, water. This, sir, is leather."*

This same year, 1954, is the year the horses are sold. The
cavalry school is now armored. National Collegiate Polo
Championship one year—the coveted Townsend Trophy.
Next year, second-rate football.

We learn manners. We learn to sit on the first three inches
of our chairs at attention while eating a square meal—straight
up from the plate, then a right angle into the mouth—and
holding a glass with the little finger and thumb while forming
a fist with the rest of the hand; and we learn to eat a meal in
three minutes. All of these things we learn while being shouted
at by old cadets who have had the privilege to be similarly
abused in past years.

There is a large, older classman. He is drunk late at night.
He has me stand stiffly at attention and lean into his hand:
down, down he takes me, almost to the floor, then SLAM up
against the wall . . . down, down, SLAM . . . down, down.
Bruised, bleeding. His name is Robert Sisk. Where are you,
Sisk? Do you know you taught me to hate at sixteen?

Leadership training and the military machine: break the
spirit, remove the personal pride, destroy the sensitivity,
restructure the body and the mind. The soul? Maybe not.
The military has the right to demand a response to orders
without question or hesitation. Battles are won that way: Iwo
Jima and San Juan Hill. And lost: Pickett's charge at
Gettysburg, Hood's charge at Franklin, Custer's charge at the
Little Big Horn, the charge of the Light Brigade on the

heights above Balaclava. Yahoo, point the saber and charge!

We have two generals at New Mexico Military Institute. The superintendent is Lt. Gen. Hobart "Hap" Gay, Patton's chief of staff throughout World War II. The commandant is Brig. Gen. John P. Willey. Both carry swagger sticks. We have contempt for swagger sticks. General Willey's is missing one day. The corps of cadets will be punished: form up, then double-time through the fresh snow of a frozen January morning until the culprit returns the stick. Run, run, most of the morning. Forget about breakfast and classes; the general's riding crop is missing. Then he finds it where he had forgotten he left it. No apology. The fresh winter air is good for young men—good preparation for cavalry attacking the Cheyenne on the Washita River. Yahoo. Point the crop and charge!

"What is the best state in the Union, Rat?"
"Sir, the state of intoxication, sir."

I spend two years in the prison for young renegades. But what I learn there—a dog learns a lot in obedience school—is in fact what probably keeps me from going to a real jail later: fear and respect for authority. Is that all that keeps a young man out of jail? Doesn't honesty, integrity, cleanness of purpose, the desire to do right, weigh heavily here? Well, yes. That and the fear of getting the shit kicked out of you. Maybe integrity is a thing you develop, a thing of philosophy. But fear is the motivating catalyst to calm a renegade.

Now, after graduation, I am loose in the weeds.

*I detect my first aroma of
wilderness here—a rich scent
of spruce, alder, kelp.*

CHAPTER THREE

Delight Creek

The sun has beaten its way back into my life. After two weeks
of wind and rain, the trip up the fjord to the glacier is a pleasure. The wind lays low, a slight sea breeze from off the bay.
Ahead, the great glacier jumps out in vibrance from the darkness of a flat water, an exaggeration of dense, shimmering
ice glowing like an alien behemoth bathing in its own source
of light.

We beach the wooden skiff, Crowley and I, climb the low
slopes of the mountain, then angle across the moraine edges
toward the open ice. Loose gravel slides for yards around us
as we near the glacier. We know we are already on the field:
ice stares out at us from only a few inches beneath the dirt
and gravel. The whole side of the hill may go to sea with us
on it, but we seem to gain a false confidence from each other,
ignoring the danger. Then, shod in our rubber hip boots, we
clamber out onto the bare ice, slick as oiled marble.

It's an overwhelming sight, standing on the edge of an ice
bridge, peering into the bowels of the glacier. White sun-
glare stabs the surface but turns to shades of blue as the eyes
work their way downward, seeking the comfort of cooler

light. The hue moderates to aquamarine, then to the dark of deep bruises, and finally to the black of yawning holes, like the sightless eyes of a hollow skull. There is a rush of water below, a rivering torrent of unseen summer melt boiling in the guts of the glacier. How long would our bodies remain entombed before the glacier released us back to a new world? Five hundred years? I'm not fearful, though. At nineteen years old, I don't have enough sense to be fearful.

In this summer of 1957, the Bureau of Commercial Fisheries of the U.S. Fish and Wildlife Service has hired most of its Alaska Territorial streamguards from the states, paying their way to Anchorage by air from Seattle. For a college student fresh out of the brown New Mexico desert, it is a free trip to a paradise of wilderness green.

On a single day in Anchorage we are indoctrinated, trying to absorb all there is to know about the commercial salmon fisheries, the laws we will enforce, first aid, survival techniques, report writing, repairing stoves and lanterns and outboard motors, and operating small skiffs on the ocean waves. Then out of Lake Hood in a twin-engine amphibian Grumman Goose: three streamguards and all our gear, with just enough room for us to lie on top of the tents, outboard motors, groceries, and baggage as we peer down through side windows at the vast coastal wilderness drifting by. There are no horizons from this angle, only a downward view into tundra, spruce, birch, lakes, and bogs; too much, and too fleeting, to impress the mind with anything more substantial than the awe inspired by a strange country.

The Kenai village airport is a dirt strip in the tundra. We bounce along in the dust and let off one man and his gear. I don't envy him; we are still in civilization. Then on to Port Dick, beyond the boardwalk village of Seldovia, where the clean sea begins to broaden. We off-load the next guy. He is luckier; I detect my first aroma of wilderness here. In an off-shore breeze, it pours through the open hatch of the bobbing Grumman—a rich scent of spruce, alder, kelp.

By late afternoon we touch down in salt spray at Nuka Bay, a pronged fjord along the outer rim of seacoast still attached to the Kenai Peninsula thumb. The pilot, a transplanted Canadian, lowers the Grumman's gear legs, dodging black rocks off the beach using the big tail rudder. With the hand/eye coordination of an artist, he alternates power between the twin 450-horsepower Pratt and Whitney radial engines as he drives the old seaplane up onto the sandy shore by the mouth of Delight Creek, my assigned post. There are no special last-minute instructions; the pilot's job is simply to get me here. Although he works for the Fish and Wildlife Service, he doesn't show much interest beyond "driving the bus." He answers my questions with grunts and shrugs and is in a hurry to get home for supper. Maybe I just want to delay being left here, or maybe I want some fanfare and praise for risking it all alone in the subarctic wilderness. Maybe I simply want my mother to tell me one more time to look both ways before crossing the street.

Moments later I stand on this wild beach, a mound of gear stacked behind me, and listen to the drone of the Grumman's engines fading into the distance. It is a lonely place. In some ways I want the sound of the plane to return. But then I think: *Wait a minute, here you are at last, out beyond the manicured lawns, out toward the culmination of dreams.*

> *Listening for the resonance of a*
> *thoughtful earth, I hear none—only*
> *surface pronouncements: wind, rivers,*
> *thunder, avalanches, rustling leaves, waves.*
> *And the deep of the earth is silent, thinking—inside,*
> *somewhere below the magma. The heart is*
> *there; I feel it the same way a bird feels it.*

MY FATHER INSPIRED the wanderlust in me, this need to make an Alaska journey. He talked about it often; about the opportunities, the lands open to homesteading, and the unlimited fishing and hunting. He spent the war years in the Aleutian Campaign: Kiska, Shemya, Attu—those barren islands of long grass, williwaws, and blue foxes, where he claimed they used log chains for wind socks and no one ventured to the latrine alone in a blizzard nor without hanging onto the ropes that led there. After the war he wanted to pull up stakes and move the family to Homer, Alaska, a favorite for servicemen in the late '40s. But the old man never made it; never even got to see it.

Now, here in 1957, not so far from Homer, I face into a kelp wind that floats off the bay and see mountains sheered steep, creased with snow. It isn't so bad to be alone, I think. I locate a spot for the tent on the lee side of a clump of alders, haul up the gear and groceries from a few hundred yards down the beach, set up the tent, and arrange things a bit. It is eleven at night, day only now turning to dusk.

I don't have any lumber, nor saw to rip it if I did, so the heavy wooden packing boxes will do for table, chair, and shelves. An army cot rounds out the furniture, and a Coleman lantern and two-burner stove will work for heat on rainy days in the eight-by-ten-foot wall tent. A five-gallon gas tin, cut open at the ends, with one end slatted with alder dowels, will serve as an ice box. Drifting chunks of ice from the glaciers are delivered on each outgoing tide, and my vegetables and meats are kept cool and fresh in this can, covered and wired outside to an alder branch.

I unpack my fishing rod and try the creek (back home, we would call it a river). First cast—Dolly Varden on! Then, one after the other, two- to five-pounders. Hog heaven. Fresh-fried char for supper, and again at breakfast. Praise be. I fish the creek each day, each hour it seems, like an addict who dreams every moment of the next fix, drunk with the need for more and without power to resist.

THERE ARE SOUNDS strange to desert ears. Rumblings, like distant thunder, drift down on the wind from the glaciers as calves of ice split away and slip into the sea as icebergs, creating their own small tidal waves. A berg coasts slowly down the bay, slipping by camp in a day or so, bound for the open Pacific, like a bright white oceanliner creeping quietly out of port for adventure on a distant sea. I've been told to be alert for ice while running the skiff; a small, clear sliver jutting up among the choppy waves may top a submerged ice chunk the size of a washtub.

New birds are here, new for me: glaucous gulls, black-hooded Bonapartes, kittiwakes, short-billed dowitchers. And one I've known before: *Corvus corax*, the common raven, waddling about with a graceful ungracefulness. But in the air he is tuned to his element, large primaries splayed out and feeling the wind like caressing fingers. He is black against the vert hills, the white sky; blacker than the blackest black, like a dark Stygian being. From somewhere across the creek, two of these birds with a sense of humor fly to my camp in early mornings to perch on the ridgepole. Taking turns, they drop small sticks and spruce cones down the sloping canvas to rattle like tiny clawed feet, each bird in turn swooshing off a short distance and coming back with another piece. It is a mischievous ritual: rattle, rattle, whoosh, whoosh, rattle . . . croak. They know they are my alarm clock. The game will end only when I give up trying to sleep and get out of bed to make coffee.

Before the first week has ended, the boats of the seine fleet begin to arrive, and two fishermen help me drag my skiff down out of the grass above the beach line. The little outboard barely pushes the skiff through the water; just enough to raise the bow, but who cares? I'm afloat—icebergs be damned! And what the hell, I can navigate over the bow just fine by standing up somewhat stooped in the stern while steering with the outboard's short handle, looking like George Washington crossing the Delaware. I navigate that way until one of the fishermen lets me know that people (mostly ignorant streamguards) drown every season after being flipped out the back of a skiff when it strikes a stringer of submerged kelp or a chunk of ice.

A SEAL HUNTER stays in a cabin across the bay, they tell me, up at the head of James Lagoon. His name is Pete Kesselring, out of Seward. I head that way early one morning.

The entrance to the lagoon is tricky for a greenhorn. When the tide is running, the narrow entrance rages like the torrent of a swollen river. But once through the half-mile rapids, I find the lagoon opens into a painting: snow-topped peaks and dark spruce trees frame the green water of the lagoon, which reaches back toward the mountains a couple of miles away. At the upper end of the lagoon, two hundred feet back from the shore, situated in a grove of spruce and along a brook of springwater, is Pete's cabin. The worn trail winds through deep moss. Pete greets me like I've been his friend forever, making me feel at home. And as it turns out, I am his friend forever, for the rest of his life.

Old Pete must be forty-five at least. He wears a large reddish beard, beginning to gray, and a big grin on a round, red, windblown face. He hunts harbor seals for a living in the summer, guides moose and bear hunters in the fall, and traps for fur in the winter. Pete is skillful with the seals, plinking them in the head with a scoped .220 rifle at twenty yards or more from a bobbing skiff. He doesn't miss often, and he knows just when to pull the trigger after the seal has taken a lung-full of air; wrong timing and the seal will sink. He picks up a three-dollar government bounty on the scalp—a bounty lobbied in by fishermen who blamed the seals for damaging nets and competing with them for salmon. He also gets five to eight dollars for a pelt.

The old cabin is a masterpiece of woodwork, with spruce logs large enough to require only four or five to a wall, and a floor fashioned of rips from the same-size trees, adzed to a hardwood sheen. Shakes for the roof are thin-split pieces from big spruce blocks.

"Old Bob built it," Pete tells me. "He was a hermit of sorts; went to town only once every year or two, and then only if he had to. Ol' Herring Pete, from Nuka Island, looked in on him now and then, once every couple of months, and brought in supplies. Bob injured his hand one day, workin' on the inboard engine of his boat. It got bad infected and finally got the gangrene. Bob figured Herring Pete wouldn't be around for another six weeks so he wrote a note explainin' the sort of fix he was in, scribbled it with his good hand, I guess, then went outside, sat down on the choppin' block, and blew the top of his head off with his aught-six. Well, as it turns out, Herring Pete showed up within two days, by the looks of things, and gets the shit scared outta hisself. Backed all the way down to the water, jumped in his boat, and headed for the U.S. Marshal's office in Seward."

I look at old Bob's calendar; it is still on the wall, turned to April 1943.

MY SURVEYS OF THE CREEKS and marking of the closed areas are on schedule when the commercial fishing season starts. The sockeye salmon are not showing in large numbers, however, and most of the seiners head elsewhere after a couple of weeks, leaving a few diehards. Among these will be the creek robbers. The salmon congregate in large schools about the mouth of a spawning creek just before migrating upstream. To ensure adequate escapement, the creek entrances are closed to fishing in most areas. The closures in the Nuka Bay area in 1957 consist of a radius of five hundred feet from the mouth of any stream used by spawning salmon. If not protected, a creek can be robbed in minutes by a purse seiner laying its net in a circle around the hundreds or thousands of fish at a stream mouth and closing the purse beneath them.

I've been suspicious of one particular seiner that hangs around just outside the closed area near my camp at Delight Creek. At one point the skipper of the seiner offers me free boat gas for a sightseeing trip to the glacier, as he knows I am low on fuel. I politely refuse. The next night he and his helpers bring their boat into the creek mouth to make a quick killing. They think I'm in bed; they haven't seen any activity since before midnight—and figure I won't be able to run them down because the low tide has beached my skiff.

They have finished a perfect set when I step out of the bushes. By then it is full daylight, sometime after three in the morning, with the sun peeking over the mountain. I snap some pictures with my Brownie box camera and signal the boat to shore, but they pull their gear without any fish and run. Another seiner chugs around the corner about that time, so I wave it in. I wade out and get on board, and we are on our way. The creek robbers stop when they see I have a ride and wait for us to catch up. I am not old enough to write a citation or make an arrest. Those of us under twenty-one can only gather evidence, so I get a written statement from the skipper, and he drops me off ashore. The photos, sketches, and testimony will convict him and his two crew members in

U.S. Commissioner's Court in Seward at the end of August.

Meanwhile the fishing in Nuka Bay has ended, and even Pete Kesselring is packing up his skiff and getting ready to head back to his wife and daughters in Seward. He stops by for a last visit and cup of coffee before heading out.

"Say, I been meanin' to tell ya," he says, "that coffee of yours sure tastes salty, and it gets worse ever time I come by."

"It tastes OK to me, Pete."

"Well, are ya sure ya ain't gettin' your water from outta the drink?"

"Sure, I'm sure," I say, "I always cut back to the creek behind camp for my drinking water. That's a good four hundred yards upstream from the mouth."

"Well, it still tastes salty to me," Pete grumbles.

I start to notice it myself a day or two after he leaves, so I take a closer look at the creek at high tide. Sure enough, I've been taking my water below the high tide mark. This late in the summer the creek is low, and the biggest part of the water draining out of it is seawater! I've been making coffee with it for a week or more.

MY WORST SCARE that summer occurs several miles down the bay and across on the other shore. I am surveying a stream for sockeyes and have foolishly secured my skiff by merely looping the bow line over a pointed boulder. The trek up the creek takes several hours longer than I intend, as I check again and again to see what is around the next bend, peering into deep pools, stuffing my cheeks with yellow salmonberries, idling along as though there were no other world. Finally I realize the tide will be well on its way in, flooding the flats where I have left the skiff. I head back at a trot.

My fear is confirmed when I round the last bend and see only a bay of water where the lower stream had wound its way through the flats. No skiff. I take a quick fix on the situation: only the clothes on my back; fjords and icefields, rock slides and alder jungles between here and the Kesselring cabin; the Goose not expected for another ten days. Even when the Goose comes, weather permitting, the pilot will think nothing of my not being in camp. I force myself to overcome a rising panic. The incoming tide will not have taken the skiff out to sea. I check the wind. A light breeze blows from out in the bay, but angles toward shore.

I retrace my route up the creek to where I can cross, then head through alders and rocks down the edge of the shore. The tide is at full flow, the sun gone behind the mountains. I feel a tinge of hunger—or is it fear? Rounding a bend, I see my skiff, waiting for me against the shoreline, resting easy. The incoming tide simply lifted the line off the rock, and the offshore breeze floated the boat a mile or so downwind. It is like finding a long-lost friend. I add up my blessings as I motor across the bay to camp.

THE WEATHER OVER the next few weeks turns sour: wind and rain, then rain and fog. Too nasty for the Goose to get in with my mail and groceries. I'm not short on the grocery end, but mail is primary. I savor the news from home; I number all the letters, reading them time and again. I have a hunger to read, but without books or magazines, tin-can labels are the most interesting reading I have, other than the letters.

When you are alone, beyond the clatter of civilization, strange sounds present themselves at odd times. The voices of men talk in the gurgles of a stream circling a boulder; faint sounds of distant motors hum in the inner ear. But this time the sound of an outboard engine is not imagined. It has been a constant murmur for forty-five minutes. I've written it off as a faint buzz in my ears, but it develops into the distinct whine of a wound-up Johnson outboard and within minutes presents itself as a true-life skiff rounding the point at full speed. It's my old New Mexico friend, Steve Crowley, streamguard from Nuka Island, a million miles away!

I haven't talked to a soul for weeks, nor have the conversations with myself been enough to prevent a show of dumbness, which surprises even me. The words erupt in jumbled, nonsensical babble as soon as the skiff noses up onto the beach. I have so much to say and cannot enunciate any of it. Crowley looks at me in studied amazement, as if I've broken wind in front of his mother. After several false starts in trying to speak, I finally have the good sense to shut up and, with great self-control, quietly listen to Crowley's end of things as we unload his gear and anchor his skiff. He is going to stay a while. The tin-can labels are suddenly unimportant.

After supper, Crowley brings in a .12-gauge Remington pump shotgun. He is proud of it. It is covered from trigger guard to muzzle with the rust of ages. Herring Pete of Nuka Island has loaned it to him for bear protection. We streamguards are not allowed to bring guns with us.

"Is it loaded?" I ask, starting to check for myself.

"No."

I point it at the ceiling and pull the trigger, blowing a neat hole the size of a half-dollar through the top of the tent. I look at him, into his blue, shocked eyes, like he is the biggest dummy I have ever known. He looks at me in the same way. Dust from the tent sifts past our pale faces. My ears are still ringing two hours later. Maybe there's good reason they don't want us to have guns.

We go on our glacier exploration the next day, and the seas are rough on the way back. It takes hours to go the ten miles or so. We are drenched and frozen, but it has been a satisfying adventure—a shared adventure. I hate to see Crowley head out the next morning; I am just beginning to get caught up on the conversation.

ALMOST TWENTY YEARS LATER, as I circle in my plane from a thousand feet up, I try to remember the topography as it had been in 1957. The big earthquake of 1964 rearranged this part of Alaska. The ground in the Nuka Bay area has settled some twenty feet. Spits, reefs, and bars are gone; the mouths of streams are displaced as much as half a mile; spruce-tree flats are now bogs, with bleached remnants of once stately spruce jabbing into the gray sky like white javelins.

I locate the Kesselring cabin, or what is left of it. I think it can't really be, but it is. After landing in the lagoon and easing my way to shore in the milky water, I tie the floatplane down and pick my way afoot across the sandy waste and fallen gray timber to the shambles of the log house, which now lies in a storm tide flat.

Mud and sand reach three feet up the walls of the old cabin, and the roof has fallen in. A muddy seep lies where the freshwater brook once ran. Nothing I can conjure up with open eyes will remind me that this was once a picturesque setting and a place of warmth. An old enameled tin plate is wedged between the logs. I brush off the dried mud, polish the enamel with my shirt sleeve. I concentrate, squinting my eyes to see inward better; maybe I can help the plate communicate, in some mystic way, what has happened here through the years. I try to absorb its memories and through it gain a connection with the past. But it isn't necessary; I realize finally that the connections with this country, the memories of this first true wilderness experience of mine, have never left me.

" . . . And green and golden I was
huntsman . . . the foxes on the hills
barked clear and cold . . ."

—Dylan Thomas
Fern Hill

PART TWO

THE DESERT

SOUTHWESTERN
NEW MEXICO

The local game warden, Roy Snyder, is easy to find most any day: he'll be at Uncle Billy's Bar, usually in the back room at the poker table.

CHAPTER FOUR

The Law West of Magdalena

In New Mexico, the old-time game wardens who set the example for us, men who had been in the business since the early 1930s and '40s, were tough in some cases but usually bighearted. If they liked you, you would learn something; if not, you were out of luck. Most of them were long on woods and wildlife savvy but short on modern law enforcement techniques. The majority of them had some unorthodox ways of catching poachers, but they were ways that worked for them, and I suppose that was good enough. Paperwork be damned, they just took 'em in, told the judge what happened, and that was that.

Luther Anthony "Bear" Turner was the game warden at the old cow town of Magdalena. Bear was tough as nails, or so he would have you think. Gruff and aggressive might best describe him. Not built like a bear exactly, although that particular nickname fit him, he was of medium height, round but solid, with a straight back and an ample gut hanging over the

43

belt, square jaw, black thinning hair, and dark eyes that squinted out from the shadow of his broad hat with a look of intelligence and kindness. He struck you that way, Turner did, intelligent and kind. Unless you were a poacher; then he struck you as intelligent and, well, intimidating. He ran his large district seated at the coffee table in the old Hammond Hotel in Magdalena—used the Hammond dining room as his main office for over twenty years—and it was a good bet you could catch him there most any day at any time, up to about ten or eleven at night. Could, anyway, until the Hammond Hotel burned down. My first thought when I heard the hotel had burned was, *What's Bear gonna do?* Well, he moved his operation across the street to the Ponderosa Cafe. Didn't miss a lick.

Old Bear was a man of legend. Stationed at Magdalena forever, he had a gift of gab and was like an old friend or uncle to thousands of hunters bottlenecking through there from the Mogollon and San Mateo mountains. He was an expected sight; they all knew him, and if they didn't, they claimed they did. He said someone once sent him a Christmas card from back East addressed: Bear Turner, New Mexico. It reached him without a hitch.

IN THAT FIRST DEER HUNTING SEASON for me as a full-time game warden, the fall of 1959, I meet Turner in the hotel dining room, there in the front lobby of the Hammond, and he outlines where he will have me patrol that day. I am disappointed we won't be together, as I'm eager to work with him; however, he says we will meet for a roadblock that evening.

He and I and three other officers meet that night on the paved highway that runs out of Magdalena. We set up a roadblock just far enough over a rise so we won't cause a traffic accident, but close enough to surprise any hunters trying to smuggle a mule deer doe home. We check scores of hunters and a lot of legal bucks before I run into something new for me as a rookie. Some guy has a field-dressed deer laid surreptitiously under a blanket behind the front seat of his car. The "buck" is properly tagged, but has no head, antlers, or other evidence of sex. The hunter is nervous. He tells me he killed the deer far back in the San Mateo Mountains that morning, but unfortunately he had shot the antlers off, and subsequently removed the head so as not to have to tote any more than necessary, but he'd be pleased to show me where all this had taken place, along with the head and antlers, and even the sex organs and gut pile, tomorrow when it was daylight, and if I had all day to hike way back in there with him . . . Bear Turner walks up about that time and asks me if there's a problem.

I tell Turner the hunter's story while he shines his flashlight around the deer and down onto the floorboards, his nose getting farther down into all of it each second, and the hunter just as curious watching over his shoulder, like he maybe wants to help Bear find whatever it is he is looking for. Pretty soon Turner picks up a small ball of deer fat, about the size of a pea. He holds it up high in front of himself, studiously peering at the glob of suet with his light, the hunter and I up close too, like curious students, peering along with him. Then—sort of low-like under his breath—he says, "An ovary."

"What?" the hunter asks, dismayed.

"An ovary, goddammit, I know an ovary when I see one!

Where'd you kill this damn doe?"

"Well, I . . . over in Spring Canyon," the startled hunter says in confession.

OLD BEAR TURNER could be tough, all right, but I heard of one time he quietly went back to a hard-luck poacher's house with groceries for the family, after taking the man to court. And there's the time he helped me pay for a trail hound but refused to take my money later; said he'd rather have half-interest in the dog. Hell, he had more dogs than he knew what to do with. It wouldn't do for anybody to make a fuss over thanking him— he would just get gruff about it.

I had sense enough to know I couldn't survive using the intimidating tactics or language that carried Bear Turner through; however, it didn't take long, working around his likes, to get a feel for things. Each of the old-timers had his own special knack for taking shortcuts to get to the root of the problem. I tried to learn a little from each of them and pick up a few of their better qualities.

I must say here that even the old-timers had their day as rookies. A case in point was a story Tom Moody, Sr., told on himself. When Tom was a young game warden just breaking in back in the early 1930s, he was sent up to Chama, New Mexico, to help the old-timer stationed there. The old warden said maybe Tom could catch "them thievin' bunch of varmints" poaching the spawning brown trout at El Vado Lake. He sent Tom down there for nighttime stakeout duty along the river just below the dam, where spawners were gathering in the closed area.

Tom, anxious to prove his mettle, jumped at the opportunity and was well-situated in the bushes overlooking the spawning area shortly after dark. The night air was chilly, and the rocks gained considerable hardness as the evening wore on. Only the sounds of the bubbling river water and the breeze in the bushes disturbed an otherwise silent vigil.

Along about midnight the long wait appeared to pay off. Down through the brush crept three or four prospective clients. They reached the river some yards below him, and shortly he could tell by the sound of fish slapping the water and the enthusiastic conversation of the poachers that they were having a successful time of it. Tom, in his excitement, kicked loose a sizable rock that went crashing down through the brush. The enthusiastic conversation became shouts of alarm as the poachers grabbed their poles and spawner trout and took off downriver.

Tom was not to be foiled. He was the law, and his authority would not be questioned. In a booming voice he commanded, "Shalt, or I'll hoot!"

The sounds of laughter were clearly audible as the anglers broke new trail bolting down through the bushes.

The old-timer never did hear the full story of what happened that night, and Tom must have had twenty-five years under his belt before he told anybody about "them thievin' bunch of varmints."

MY FIRST PERMANENT ASSIGNMENT to a one-man post is the Reserve District, the largest in the state. It lies within the bounds of Catron County, the largest and least populated county. It is my introduction to the Gila Forest, the Mogollon Mountains in the center: prime country for turkeys, black bears, mountain lions, mule deer, and elk, with grassland pockets of pronghorn antelope. The forest comprises the high headwater lands of the Gila and San Francisco rivers, with the upper reaches of these rivers and their tributaries forming the Gila Wilderness.

I have a month to work with the local game warden, Roy Snyder, and learn the ropes before he retires. He knows the country well, having been born and raised here. Roy is easy to find most any day: he'll be at Uncle Billy's Bar in the town of Reserve, usually in the back room at the poker table, in uniform, a glass of bourbon at hand. His patrol truck is parked out front. That way you know he is there. It is seldom the truck is not there.

Roy, who is sixty-seven, put in a full career with the U.S. Forest Service before joining the Game and Fish Department as a mountain lion hunter about 1944. He has been district warden at Reserve for over ten years. When I get settled in, I ask Roy for the district files. He gives me a partially used purchase order book full of old dog and horse feed receipts and an envelope full of various blank forms. I have been anxious to take a look at what I think will be a sizable array of files on past game surveys, correspondence, and violation records.

"Would there be anything else that I'll be getting, Roy?" I ask.

"Why, shore," he says. "Thar's the old single-horse trailer. You can pick it up any time. Might want to slap some new paint on it, though."

"OK . . . but are there any other files or papers to go with the district? I mean, like a lot of the old stuff, you know."

"Nope." And there is a silent period as he looks at me methodically, perhaps to see if I want to pursue the question further or maybe misunderstood his explanation.

"You see," he says, "thar's nothin' but that book. I don't do much writin' . . . just the reg'lar reports on mileage and such as that." Roy speaks slowly when he speaks at all, and in a deep voice that rumbles up from down inside somewhere. He is gaunt and tanned and has large bony fingers that rest easy until he surprises you with a quick gesture. "As far as stuff from the head office and such as that, well I just hold them envelopes up to the light," he says, as he holds up his empty hand, "and if thar ain't a check in thar, why I just toss 'em in the trash." He makes a quick gesture with his arm, from up against the living room lamp where he is pretending to be peering through an envelope, down to a wastebasket. He does not say this in humor, nor with any disgust, just as a fact. I accept his explanation as the end of the matter, and it is just as well: he has done all the explaining he is going to do.

Roy: tall, rawboned, sun-beaten, windblown old game warden, forest ranger, cowboy, trapper, lion hunter, World War I veteran. He has led a life heavy with the wild adventures most of us only read about. His established position at that point is not easy for me as a young officer to understand: he is tired of the new bureaucratic scheme of things, he is ready to make his rest official, and he is comfortable with what he is.

I don't know why they didn't just call us cow wardens and be done with it. We killed wildlife for the sake of the cow.

CHAPTER FIVE

Predators

Shorty Lyon—squat, round, and silver-haired—lived up on a mountain above the old silver-mining ghost town of Mogollon, in Catron County, where in addition to his trapping chores, he was caretaker of a long-dormant silver diggings—the Fanny Mine. Old weathered-gray frame houses were perched on the sides of the mountains there at the Fanny, a scene straight out of a Snuffy Smith comic. You could sit on Shorty's front porch and look right down on the long, snaking road that climbed through the town, and even see straight down onto the main street where boarded-up old stores sat along the creek bottom. You could see so well from there, in fact, that one day Shorty's wife, sitting on the porch with her neighbor, said, "I wonder who that woman is with Shorty?" as they peered down at Shorty's truck winding its way up the road far below. Shorty later admitted he had a female with him all right. It was Minnie Belle, his favorite old black-and-tan hound, riding up in the front seat instead of in the back with the rest of the dogs.

Like most of the government hunters of his day, Shorty Lyon was a houndman, with some of the finest lion and bear dogs in the Southwest. His stories and adventures were legend, and you could always count on the fact that a good yarn would include one or more of his favorite dogs.

Some of Shorty's best tales were those where the joke was on himself. He was once stranded overnight at the old Lynx Cabin in the Mogollon Mountains, where he found only bacon grease and powdered cereal for him and the dogs to eat. The combined concoction bubbled and foamed as it heated on the old woodstove. Although it didn't taste too good, Shorty forced himself to eat a fair amount of it. The dogs wouldn't touch their share. He soon found out why as he spent most of the night running to the outhouse and back. The "powdered cereal" was some sort of powdered soap. Shorty said the so-called dumb animal in this story was clearly not a dog.

A dog is a dog, they say, but I don't believe it. There are as many personalities and levels of love, loyalty, and intelligence in dogs as in people. We all have had our favorite dogs. For me, at least in the hunting variety, it was a small bluetick hound I called Ol' Blue. She was a small, skinny dog—pure trail hound—not reared to the sounds of kindness nor accustomed to pats on the head when I got her. Nevertheless she had a gentleness and understanding in her demeanor, almost like she had been destined for a life more refined but had somehow been misdirected to a future of hard toil through river brush and mountain cactus, interspersed with long periods chained to a stake in a dog lot. She was leery of any kindness, but not in the skittish manner of an abused alley cat. With a quiet attitude she simply accepted any kindness as an agreeable but unnecessary act by the masters of her assignments, if not of her soul.

My kids were attracted to Ol' Blue, although she was an unkempt, bony old thing with coarse, wiry hair and an ugly vacant eye kicked out in her younger, less cautious days by a wild-natured mule. She had a lovely heart and a soft yodel to her mournfully mouthed howl, and she expressed a loyalty from out of that one good eye. She was tolerant of the kids examining her long, loose ears, ragged and split at the ends from too many 'coon fights along the river bosques, and accepting of them sitting on her as she lay in the shade of her doghouse, as if they were her own brood. Though slight of build, she was tough on the trail, an unrelenting hunter of 'coons, bears, and mountain lions.

The need to hunt courses through canine veins, and if bred and trained to pursue, they will live for that experience; they'll be unhappy without it. Maybe it is the same for some people.

TO SHORTY LYON'S WAY of figuring, every coyote or mountain lion killed meant several deer or elk saved, and every fox trapped was one less threat to game-bird nests. But he didn't trap or hunt with a vengeance or with malice toward the hunted. He had a sincere respect for the "predatories," as he called them, and in most cases put them in a class much higher than the two-legged human predator.

Shorty and I once came upon a female red fox in one of his traps back up on 916 Mesa, along the western slope of the Mogollons, and we could see that she was lactating and probably had a den of hungry pups somewhere near. She was not seriously hurt, so Shorty turned her loose; said he didn't want to run out of foxes to catch, so maybe it was a good idea to turn one loose every now and then. Maybe he was just preserving the stock to ensure himself a job. Or maybe not.

Most of the West is livestock country to one degree or another; at least the livestock owners laid claim to it early on. And the ranchers quickly discovered which animals they wanted to have around and which they didn't. The undesirable predator, the wild animal with a taste for the very things we humans like, is bound to end up with the short stick, whether this predator is a hungry vixen after quail on 916 Mesa or a black bear with a liking for cow meat, like the bear we trapped out of the Burro Mountains southwest of Silver City.

There's not much water in the Burros. You go up a dry sandy wash where there are big oak trees fat with green foliage, and they look as though they are happily thriving along a freshwater river. You expect to see water, but there's just more sand, rocks, and hot sun around each bend. There are a handful of springs in the Burros, but each one is a creeping seep—a damp spot venturing up out of the sand and then disappearing a few feet beyond, as though realizing its mistake in popping up in the middle of such a place, and so, quickly retreats to find another entrance a thousand miles away. And you think there must be something more substantial farther on—but another side of you knows better.

We trapped our bear not far from one of these springs. We took it with a No. 15 Victor, a big steel-jawed double-spring trap you have to compress with C-clamps (you leave the clamps with the armed trap in case some unsuspecting soul discovers what it's like to have a heavy, unforgiving trap, chain, and drag anchored to his ankle or wrist with no way out). Power to crush a big bone. Offset teeth to pierce the hide and to hang on like raptor talons.

Jack Jolly, an old swizzle-necked cowboy, and I rode horseback in to check on a yearling Hereford heifer Jack said was killed by this bear. The day before, Jack had been trailing up a little bunch of cows and had to detour around a rough draw, but when he intercepted the cows at the upper end there was one missing. Back-trailing into the draw he came upon the yearling with her jaws ripped open. She was still alive, standing like she was simply awaiting her fate, but unable to bawl with her tongue missing and not wanting to move for who knows why. Jack put her out of her misery with his saddle carbine, checked the mingle of cow and bear tracks, and got out of there.

Bears prefer to eat the tender parts of a cow first. They usually eat the tongue and udder bag, then leave the rest to rot, for reasons known only to the scrupulous taste of a bear—rotten to the point of being swarmed over by maggots, anyway; then it becomes a delicacy. That's the condition best describing the carcass of the heifer when the bear returned and stepped into the No. 15 Victor.

The old bear was up in one of those healthy valley oaks when I made my daily check—up there off the hot sand of the dry wash, trying to shake the steel trap off a numb forefoot. One of my sons was with me. He was six years old—a time to have the honor of killing a bear, I thought. We crouched below the tree and I helped him line up the sights on the .30-.30 carbine, bracing the rifle myself, and let him pull the trigger. The old bear flinched, and sagged, then began to moan. The low wail came from deep inside and sounded to me like the pained lamentation of an old man, the sounds of grief he might make when struck by tragic news. The wail caused the hair on the nape of my neck to tingle, and I quickly killed it with another shot.

The moan of that bear was stamped on my conscience to last a lifetime, and although my little boy was silent as to the effect, I felt a tremor through his body at the sound. Later, when he was a grown man, I asked if he recalled killing the bear in the tree. He said he remembered it clearly, but could not recall the moan, only shooting the bear.

I TRIED TO UNDERSTAND, to justify if I could—at least for myself—our control of predators. The trapping we did was almost entirely for the cattleman and the sheepman. We tried to be sure that the bear caught feeding on a dead cow was actually the bear that had killed it. I suppose that was the case part of the time, but even so, who the hell cares, other than the guy who owns the cow? It wouldn't do for me to have to make the decision now, whether or not to kill a stock-killing bear. I get tired of stepping on cow shit in bear country, if you know what I mean.

Coyotes. I think about the coyotes I took with steel traps and cyanide guns. There was a time I took pride in such killing, for reasons of "game protection." But it was really stock protection: protecting the cow from the wildlife— eagles, wolves, bears, and coyotes—and from animals competing for the forage—deer, elk, bison, and prairie dogs. We set the hunting season bag limits based largely on the carry-ing capacity of the range—range over-grazed and over-browsed by livestock. I don't know why they didn't just call us cow wardens and be done with it. We killed wildlife for the sake of the cow. And not for just a few years, but from the time the first cattle barons took over the free land out West (once the Indians and the buffalo had been eradicated). We are still killing wildlife for the sake of the cow in many areas.

I have visions of a coyote in a No. 3 Victor double-spring steel trap—one of mine—out on the desert west of Las Cruces. Of the dozens I took over the years, I have visions of that particular coyote because he wagged his tail when I walked up to kill him. I do not recall any cow ever wagging her tail at anything but a fly.

But there wasn't a finer woodsman or better judge of game habitat than the old state trapper. In spite of the growing controversy over control of predators, he felt a deep commitment to his usefulness as a protector of the game animal against what he thought of as the four-legged poacher. Generally he had respect for all wildlife. But to confuse respect with kindness would not be totally accurate in this particularity.

The old-time state-hired hunter was a professional in the use of dogs and traps when the four-legged predator was high on the list of priorities for control throughout the country. In the 1940s and early '50s the New Mexico Game and Fish Department beefed up its hunter/trapper ranks by hiring the best they could find. It was the rule more often than not to start new employees out in the predator section to determine their worth. If they could handle a nomadic existence centered around dogs, traps, horses, pack panniers, and tent camps—and could apply their knowledge of wildlife and woods while working compatibly with ranchers and sportsmen alike—then, and only then, could they think about moving into the higher paying status of game warden. Most of the old-time wardens started out that way. Some, like Shorty Lyon and Walter

Rodgers, chose to stick with their traps and dogs, which they believed were the ultimate tools in protecting the deer, antelope, and elk.

Walt Rodgers' bailiwick was the sand hill, shinnery oak country of eastern New Mexico. Every road, trail, and cow path in that part of the Staked Plains—*El Llano Estacado*—was charted in his mind. A transplanted Texas cowboy, he had trapped for the state since the early '40s. Walt: "If I wasn't trailin' a trap drag, makin' a set, or huntin' for a good spot to catch a coyote, I'd feel plumb lost."

Walt had raised a herd of kids and taught them a wealth of lore about survival in the outdoors. "Those kids were raised on beans and cottontail rabbits," he would say. "We never could afford much else. And they've lived in tents and shacks along the trapline all their young lives; never lived in a permanent home, or what you would say was permanent. But then, there's a heap they can tell you about coyotes, bobcats, and the ways of a deer. And they'll surely never go hungry for the lack of not knowin' how to survive—at least as long as they can find their way into the hills."

He was in his sixties when I knew him. Tall, slightly stooped, white hair like picked cotton, blue eyes bloodshot from too many years in the bright sun and blowing sand. He wore a hearing aid, the only kind they had then: a round, black box plugged into his ear, with a wire running out of it down to his shirt pocket. There was slow movement in his manner at all times—slow, but purposeful. I recall a wisdom in Walt's eyes. I've seen it since, in old dogs, old horses, old wolves. Something that says, "I've seen it—so will you if you survive long enough—but I won't try to tell you about it; discover it in your own way."

*Barney realizes the inhumanity of
leaving anyone in his jail; therefore
he leaves the door unlocked.*

CHAPTER SIX

The Catron County Jail

The Reserve District is one of the best big-game areas in New Mexico, and I look forward to the influx of hunters in November. I want some action; the country is too laid-back for the likes of a young game warden with surplus energy. Although there is some good fishing in the district, it is too distant from any city of size to attract many people, and the deer hunting season is about the most excitement produced during the year.

Deer hunters from the Zuni reservation are working their way down into the Jewett Gap country north of Apache Creek. My concern as a game warden during this fall of 1960 is their efficiency. When they go hunting, it is serious business. If a truckload of, say, eight hunters comes into an area, it means four camps, not one. They drive as far back off the road as possible, then spread out over several hundred yards throughout the sagebrush and piñon trees with the four little camps. Each camp will have a small wickiup of brush, a campfire, and a couple of blankets.

It means a sizable amount of tracking just to locate the camps to see what they have hanging in the trees in the way of game. Multiply it all by a multitude of pickups scattered around the country and you've got yourself a workout. Not only that, some of the hunters were not above shooting whatever they come across—elk, deer, turkeys—without regard to season or bag limit. And who knows, maybe they needed the meat. But of course the country couldn't support that sort of killing and still leave any game for the city boys to take.

Late one afternoon, while working out a maze of tracks, I find three of these small camps, all connected with one pickup, and all in violation of one law or another. No one is in camp, and there is no way to watch all three places at the same time. So I load up the four deer, two turkeys, and the hindquarters of an elk in the back of my pickup and retreat to where the tracks all join together, and I wait them out. By an hour or so after dark, five of the men and one woman have shown up by trailing the vehicle that has taken their game. We build a big fire and wait for the one remaining hunter, but by about eleven I decide he is not going to come in. I take two of the men in the front of my truck and ask the others to follow in their truck. We head for old Judge Russell's court in Reserve, about fifty miles away. Outside of having a flat tire— I have no volunteers to help unload the pile of game on top of the spare tire, change the flat, and load it all back on—outside of that, and leaving my good flashlight alongside the highway, the trip is uneventful.

By the time we get to Justice of the Peace John Russell's cabin on the edge of town it must be two in the morning, and the judge is not too happy about being rooted out of the feathers. By the time Mrs. Russell gets the fire stoked up and the complaint book is filled out, it is close to three. In his eighties, with coal black hair, the judge spends most of his time seated in front of the fireplace (about the only position I ever see him in). He carries a shawl, or blanket, wrapped around his shoulders, and his attention is centered on the flickering fire. I fill out the complaint in the docket book and carry it over for him to sign. He is seated in such a way that neither he nor the defendants can look at each other; in fact, I don't recall the old judge ever seeing a defendant I bring in.

He puts on his reading glasses and studies the complaint. "Says here one of you killed an elk out o' season," he grumbles.

Only one of the Zunis speaks English, and he serves as interpreter. "Yes," he says.

"That'll be a hundred dollars fine and five dollars court costs," the judge orders.

Each complaint is handled in the same manner. Having no funds at hand, the defendants are remanded to the Catron County jail. Court stands adjourned. The deputy sheriff is called out to open the place. The jail is not a modern facility. It is a one-room adobe structure with a door, a paneless, barred window, two cots, nothing else. No lights, no toilet. The prisoners take one look at the "facilities" provided at the little adobe jail and suddenly it turns out they all seem to be fluent in English, wanting to know how long they have to be in there and so forth. I can understand their concern. It is decided that the "interpreter" will take the truck for a quick trip home for money to pay the fines. He and the woman are the only ones in the group not served with a complaint.

The woman, who is the wife of one of the defendants,

demands in her quiet way to stay in the jail with her husband. I am satisfied to see that the deputy sheriff is leaving the door of the jail unlocked as usual. It's an inhumane place even with the door open. They are all bailed out of there by supper time.

ONE OTHER THING about this Catron County jail, before I forget it: Burro Joe is to blame for bringing it into statewide focus and making it famous. Joe was considered an outsider, having been in the county for only twenty-five years or so. You have to be born in Catron County to be considered a member of the clan. He also didn't fit the profile of any of the main groups in the county. If you are not into ranching or sawmilling, then you are most likely a schoolteacher, or a preacher, or on welfare, or an employee of the U.S. Forest Service. However, Burro Joe is none of these, which may be to his credit. Joe is just reclusive, living in a shack back in the Mogollon Mountains. He does a little prospecting and occasionally works as a handyman down at the state fish hatchery in Glenwood when he needs grocery money.

Burro Joe is not an old man, maybe forty, and has the good habit of minding his own business, mostly. Joe stands maybe six feet tall and is large-boned but thin. He has a lengthy, unkempt beard and dark, sad eyes, made huge by thick, smoky-lensed glasses. He wears comfortable, baggy clothes not washed often.

If Joe poaches a deer now and then he is discreet about it, and I never know of it. But then, I have plenty of things to do other than to snoop around Joe's place. Joe does poach a cow once, though—his downfall. They call it cattle rustling in this part of the world. He gets caught in the act by the rancher whose brand is on the steer and is subsequently jailed. That might have been the end of the story if Joe had been only a couple of miles farther south when he butchered the beef, across the line toward Silver City, in an ordinary county. But Catron County is not ordinary.

The Catron County jail is located just outside the town of Reserve, the county's largest settlement and the seat of government. The town has a movie theater—usually a movie is shown there Saturday afternoon and Saturday night—and there is a cafe, bar, and grocery store. And a filling station.

Barney is the sheriff of Catron County. Everyone calls him by his first name, and I don't remember his last. Barney realizes the inhumanity of leaving anyone for long in his jail; therefore, he leaves the door unlocked. That way the incarcerated person can step outside, around behind the building, to take care of his (or her) toilet business, since a bucket is the only bathroom fixture. It also means that meals don't have to be delivered to the inmates, the county not having a budget for extra help to handle such duties; the deputy sheriff is the only employee besides Barney, and the deputy is needed for other work. So the inmates walk down to the cafe in the middle of town for their meals. It is at this jail that the cattle rustler Burro Joe is being held while awaiting trial.

It is well understood by Joe (Barney has told him the rules) that he is not to leave the jail except to eat or to get a haircut or to go to the movie on Saturday night. Any absence beyond that will be considered a serious breach of the trust given him by the county. Joe is apparently satisfied with this arrangement—at least until an armed-robbery suspect from

Arizona is moved in with him. The state policeman for this area has placed the Arizonan in the Catron County jail pending extradition proceedings and has requested that Barney maintain the suspect under lock and key. This is not workable for Barney, for all the reasons previously discussed; however, it turns out the robbery suspect is a model prisoner, really dependable about returning to the cell when he is supposed to. But it seems there is a personality conflict between Burro Joe and his Arizona cellmate, so Joe decides to leave. When the deputy checks the jail one night after making his town rounds, Joe is not there.

"Where's Joe?" he asks, casting his light about the little adobe cell, looking in the same corners more than once as if he may have overlooked Joe the first time around.

"He left early yesterday," replies the robbery suspect.

When Allen Williams, the state policeman, hears about the jailbreak (it is headlined as such in the newspapers), he heads for Reserve with great haste, his immediate concern being the possible escape of his robbery suspect. On the U.S. highway between Glenwood and Reserve, Allen notices a roadblock up ahead. The sheriff has deputized several members of the citizenry to help in the manhunt for Joe. Allen thinks he recognizes one of the deputies signaling him to stop. It is his Arizona prisoner, complete with badge and gun.

Allen does not have time to discuss the matter with Barney at that moment. Allen is busy turning around and heading back south for the Grant County jail in Silver City with his man in handcuffs, sans gun and badge.

There is a great to-do over this jailbreak for several days. Doors all over the county are locked for the first time; an escapee is on the loose. Then someone suggests we check at

Burro Joe's shack back in the hills. Well, Joe is there, of course, minding his own business, sitting out on the front stoop as we cautiously approach. His rifle is leaning against the wall, and Allen Williams asks him not to touch it. Joe says he doesn't plan to. Sad-eyed Joe has not a mean bone in him.

The mountain lion's eyes widen to
black roundness as he focuses on me.
Maybe we both feel we no longer
have control of our destiny.

CHAPTER SEVEN

The Killing Tree

There is an old black-and-white photo, eight-by-ten, taken in
1960; taken there on one of the dirt backstreets of
Magdalena. There is a pickup truck in the center, and behind
it you can see a patrol truck, green '59 Chevy with a little red
light on top, and behind that, in the background, the
Magdalena Mountains—but they are not in the far distance;
you can see their definition, and the outline of ponderosa
pines along a broken ridgeline. But your eyes are not drawn
to any of that; your eyes are drawn to the stock rack on the
back of the pickup in the center, where a dead mountain lion
hangs snubbed to the pipe-and-spruce crossbars by a rawhide
catch rope—hung by the neck like Tom Horn (though without a fair trial) and reaching seven feet, nine inches from nose
to tip of tawny tail. That is the first thing you really see, and
then there are the trail hounds, standing around in a semi-
circle, looking at the camera: Ol' Blue (she once had a litter of
twenty-three pups), Jake, Lobo, Bob, and I forget the other
one's name, Butch maybe. There are a couple of young men
in the photo, too; cowboys, squatted down, holding on to the
dogs, looks of accomplishment in their eyes. You've seen the

look before in most pictures of hunters with their bagged trophies. It isn't a look of smugness or conceit, and it doesn't have an air of haughtiness about it. The guys in those pictures always have that look of the football player in the old days who has made a touchdown, but casually drops the ball and walks away like he really hasn't done anything all that great, but still really knows he has.

Owning and hunting hounds can be addictive; dog-poor, they say. A man with a pack of good trail hounds is admired, much like someone with a good team of sled dogs in Alaska. Admired by all but the neighbors, anyway.

It is in a hound's blood and very being to hunt. Man has made sure of it in the cultivation of the breed. Some say it is inhumane not to hunt a hound. The same might be said for the houndman. What makes a houndman tick; why does he need the chase? One thing is certain: he and the hound are in tune with each other. But it is seldom he considers the plight of the hunted. Like the hound, his awareness is bent toward capture of the prey.

IN THE LATE WINTER OF 1960, they—the men in the photo at Magdalena—are hunting the Datil Mountains, a low range of yellow pine ridges along the northern edge of the San Augustine Plains in west-central New Mexico. They are hunting mountain lions, cutting for sign along ridge tops, canyon bottoms, and saddled passes in between. They are into their third day of hard riding with horses without striking fresh sign. It is February, but the only mark of a passing winter is an occasional dusty snowbank in the shadow of an outcropping or under a protected limestone rimrock. The weather has warmed toward midday and the sun feels strong along the south slopes of the ridges, releasing the fragrance of ponderosa pine, piñon, and red cedar into the wind. There are no springs or creeks along the canyon bottoms. They drink from small puddles of snow water in the dry washes and can see by the tracks and murkiness that the thirsty dogs have lapped there ahead of them.

An abundance of mule deer makes the Datils good mountain lion country. It is a natural passing-through area where a cat can make a kill without much effort while on a circuit of a hundred miles or so from one range of mountains to another. Many of the female mountain lions seem to prefer to raise their cubs in the mild-winter country of the Datils.

On this day the hunters have five dogs, of which only two have any hunting experience. It is shirtsleeve warm as they climb a high ridge and the younger dogs jump a mule deer doe, the first excitement of the day. The men cannot holler them back; the dogs are excited after many miles of inactivity; their chop and bawl fades into the distance. The two older hounds cower behind the horses, fearing punishment for getting involved with deer, which they have been broken from running long ago. That is when they cross the lion track without knowing it. The scent is fresh in the pine needles, but goes unnoticed by the older dogs due to the distractions.

On the south slope of a cedar ridge the men take a break, resting the horses and building a coffee fire. Two of the deer runners have returned, but the young bluetick named Jake has not yet given up the chase. They can hear him bawling in the distance now and then, when the breeze is right. Dry pine knots are building into a hot enough fire for coffee when they detect a change in Jake's barking. The far-off bawling has settled to a chopping bark, the familiar sound of a trail hound barking "treed." They consider the fact that this dog does not have a deer up a tree. If he had bayed the deer, the barking would have carried a different concern and pitch—a confrontational sound.

They grab up the coffee pot, kick dirt on the fire, mount up, and waste no time working their way across the ridges toward the barking hound in the distance. They find the bluetick along the edge of a yellow sandstone rimrock; he is excited under a tall ponderosa pine as a large male mountain lion walks the upper limbs. Sun reflection shines off the tawn of the lion's hide as he paces a branch nervously, hiss-spitting at the barking dogs and occasionally glancing toward the men as they ride up.

It is the beginning of the end for him. Ironically, it is also the beginning of the end of the government hunter. In 1960 the Department of Game and Fish is changing its concepts regarding control of the mountain lion. The job of state trapper and district game warden will no longer include the hunting of these cats on government time. Where once a state hunter was furnished good dogs, dog feed, groceries, and equipment for the constant pursuit of deer-killing and stock-killing lions, hunting while on duty will now cost a suspension in pay. The Department has sold the last of its hounds and has transferred all its hunters to other duties. The game manager's picture of the lion as a predator is changing. He no longer believes the lion to be a detriment to a healthy deer population. It is a difficult idea to understand in those days. Mountain lions kill many deer: Is it not the job of game protectors to capture poachers and kill lions?

"We can't shoot him now!" one of the men shouts over

the commotion. Referring to the need for the other dogs to experience the chase, he yells, "The other dogs haven't earned him yet, and these young dogs don't even know what it's all about!"

"Maybe we can climb the tree and scare him out," the other says. The steady yapping of the five dogs almost drowns him out.

"That may be the way to go, but it's a high climb without any handholds to speak of. You want to try it?"

"Who, me? What'll I do when I get up there?"

"Take a stick with you. Pound it on the trunk. He won't be able to stand it. He'll come out."

I climb high and peer into the cat's eyes from about eight feet beneath him. That is as close as I dare to get. Being up here in the ponderosa with him, far from the ground, is uncomfortable. I don't like high places, anyway. The lion looks at me not with fear, nor hatred, but more with contempt. Hissing and spitting, he reaches one foot down toward me and rests it on a lower branch. Our eyes meet, and I feel an interchange; the vertical pupils of the cat's eyes widen to black roundness as he focuses on me. Maybe we both feel we no longer have control of our destiny. But only one of us knows he is out of his element; it is not a brave thing I do— the lion is the one with the courage here. The manner in which he peers at me makes me feel insignificant, yet he seems more concerned with the dogs barking below than with me here, just beneath him, pounding a gray pine branch against the trunk and hollering like a fool.

There comes to me then a strange sensation, not unlike the uneasiness you felt when you were a child and had joined the group in picking on some other kid. But somehow you got carried away with it all and found yourself up front, facing the kid. And suddenly the kid looked bigger, and you realized at that moment, with all the other kids watching, that you were going to get the slobbers slapped out of you.

The intensity and intelligence of this animal's gaze makes me feel out of place. I wonder if I can back out without losing face. The lion is not about to move out of the tree from that height without being able to travel farther down the trunk, and I am in his way. The cat urinates on me. Maybe it is from fear—likely it is—or from the contempt he holds for me. There is no protection from it; only my hat and free arm, the one with the branch. I retreat, at ease with the thought that I now have good reason to back down.

With the report of the .38 revolver and the ripping of the slug in the branch under his foot, the lion has had enough and decides to make his break. He now has a clear path as he claws down the trunk of the yellow pine headfirst for about fifteen feet, streaks along a lengthy limb, and leaps out over the edge of the rimrock into a snowbank on the steep-sided slope far below. He bounds down through the timber and out of sight, with five excited, howling trail hounds in hot pursuit, their bawling clamor echoing off the opposite canyon walls. We scramble for our horses and hurriedly pick our way off the steep mountainside.

No more than half a mile down the canyon the dogs have the tom treed again. He has selected a small piñon tree this time. Here is a hundred and forty pounds of wiry mountain lion, capable of downing a grown bull elk by snapping its neck. Here, nervous in the piñon, is an animal who could run us all off with some aggression on his part but who suffers the age-old fear of the canine. The bullet from a revolver brings instant death as it enters the skull just forward of the left ear. From a fall of ten feet the cat strikes the ground as dead weight and the dogs are instantly there, mauling and pulling at the limber carcass.

IT WAS NOT MY LAST HUNT with hounds. The craving to hunt was a natural predatory urge. I was tuned to the dogs, they to me. But there was also a tuning in to the hunted. I did not know what it was then that I felt; the blood circulated strongly within for the want of the hunt. But somewhere I had begun to question the ethics of running down animals to kill—any animal. Was it from my early days of those first outings: mesmerized by a fleeing coyote, and forgetting to shoot; concentrating on a flock of wild turkeys, absorbed by the excitement of their presence and allowing them to escape? The need to chase would remain, but I would feel a certain uncivilized satisfaction that I was no longer comfortable with. If the hunt was a successful one, there was nothing at the end but an animal's violent death.

We tried to justify it in our minds, we houndmen. We claimed to be ridding the country of varmints: the egg-sucking raccoon, the poultry-snatching fox, the pheasant-killing bobcat, the deer-killing lion, the stock-killing bear. In truth we were in it for sport.

Houndmen are crazy. I can rightfully say that because I was crazy right along with them. The difference is, I broke away from it, matured out of it, while many of them kept the addiction for life. Dog-poor. Let the kids eat baloney but buy the best feed you can get for a yard full of dogs; live in a loose shack where the wind slams all the doors throughout the middle of the house, but worry about the comfort of Ol' Blue out front (a good houndman keeps his dogs in the front yard where people coming up to the house can admire all of them before they get to the door).

A houndman friend of mine would take four or five of his favorite dogs along with his wife and five kids when they went for a Sunday drive, all of them together inside a '55 Chevy sedan. It is true. He figured he should spend a little time with his family; besides, the best 'coon hunting was at night, so he wasn't losing any good hunting on Sunday afternoon anyway.

When I went to work for the Game and Fish Department, the bread-and-butter crop in New Mexico was the mule deer. Economically it was considered good business to control or remove anything or anyone detrimental to these deer. The Department's budget was based solely on monies derived from hunting and fishing licenses; the big money came from deer hunting licenses. Coyotes and mountain lions did not contribute to the budget. If you wanted one or more of these, you could go out and kill them; you were helping to protect the bread-and-butter crop. But by the early '60s state trappers were on the way out; the lion hunters were gone. Only certain selective trapping remained, most of it to protect the rancher's beef or mutton. Certain questionable values continued, but different values were also surfacing.

IN THE DATILS IN 1960 I contemplate this dead mountain lion. I realize that the hunt had ended before the shot was fired—had ended at the tree after the chase, when the dogs had their quarry cornered without means of escape. It had ended when the confidence of the hounds under the tree said it was over, and the eyes of the quarry, seeing all—but reflecting the dilemma of no escape—told us the same. I stand there looking and try to feel some triumph. The hunt has been a need, it seems; the short chase, exciting. I want to feel elation at the killing tree. There are centuries in our blood. I think back to the two of us in the ponderosa pine on the ridge. High in the tree, with but a few feet of space between us, there was thought in his live eyes. Now the shade drifts in. We are left by a sun gone behind the mountain.

I leap into my car to give chase.
They head south over the dirt road at
speeds in excess of seventy, training
both spotlights back at me.

CHAPTER EIGHT

Night Lights

We called them spotlighters. In certain other parts of the country, they call them jacklighters or shiners, people who hunt and kill animals at night by aid of an artificial light—mostly deer. More elk would be killed in New Mexico that way, but elk have a tendency to move away from a light and not stand and stare back. Deer will stand and stare, the green reflection of their eyes glowing back at the spotlighter. The use of a light for night hunting apparently didn't originate with the invention of the incandescent bulb. John Burroughs, the nature essayist, wrote of using a "jack" to help in killing a deer in 1863. The device was a three-candle affair mounted on a pole, with a section of birch bark placed behind to reflect the light.

Most of us stationed in deer country spent a considerable amount of time hunting spotlighters. A game warden learns all the roads and trails to perfection; it is important to know where a spotlighter's vehicle is going to come out or if it will have to return the same way it went in. I often used fire look-out towers—you could see the flash of a spotlight for thirty or more miles—and from these lookouts, in the black of night, you needed to know the country in order to figure out which road the light was coming from to plan an interception. In some areas of sagebrush and in piñon-juniper country, a large scope of acreage could be watched from a single perch on a high knoll. I drank lots of coffee sitting on high knolls most of many a night.

In order to not be spotted ourselves while traveling the back roads at night, we often drove without lights, and we had a switch on the dash for cutting off the brake lights. On a moonlit night, driving this way was a cinch; on black nights it could be disastrous. I once emerged from out of the dark like a ghost into the yellow brightness of a hunters' camp beside the road. Impressed, the hunters asked how I could manage to see in the dark. I felt the strength of their admiration and gave a dissertation on how I surreptitiously slipped up on night hunters in the act of poaching.

Then I left without lights, the same way I entered, fading into the blackness like an apparition. But the light of the campfire had blinded me, and as I drove into the darkness I couldn't see beyond the dash. I stubbornly refused to turn on the headlights (how could I? The hunters were watching, you know) and I ran through a signpost at a curve in the road, tearing the big post from its roots, and all of this less then a hundred feet from the camp. I switched on the lights, backed out (did you ever have the feeling that all eyes and thunderous laughter are directed at you, without actually seeing or hearing anything?), and hurriedly went on down the road, hoping the hunters wouldn't remember my name or recognize me if they ever saw me again.

We didn't have to catch poachers actually killing a deer. The New Mexico statutes were specific against "anyone who casts the rays of an artificial light in a game or livestock area . . . while in the possession of a firearm . . ." This was enough to make a ticket or arrest stick, and many deer (and livestock, I suppose) were saved by the strictness of it.

I WAS INVOLVED IN PLENTY of spotlighting arrests, but the one that usually pops into mind is the one at Ute Mountain, north of Taos. I learned some lessons there. Whenever I was home, which was not often, it was at the small village of San Cristobal, fifteen miles north of Taos, a picturesque spot with a view of the upper Rio Grande Gorge and sage flats to the west and the Sangre De Cristo Mountains to the east. I had a pasture for my mules, and the kids had plenty of room to mill around.

On this particular night I get a call about midnight on the radio from patrolman Lee Cordova. Someone is spotlighting up around Ute Mountain, about forty miles north of San Cristobal and up near the Colorado line. Lee is working the back roads, without his lights, trying to get close to them. I head out.

When I get up there I look out across the flats and see the light working the edge of the piñon breaks. I have radio contact with Lee, and it's agreed that I will go into Colorado, cross to the little town of Garcia, and work south toward the light. This might prevent the poachers from escaping to the north.

About the time I get through Garcia and start without lights down the gravel road leading south, Lee calls and says he is stuck in a ditch. I am closer to the spotlighters than to Lee, so I go for them first.

They are driving a '59 Ford sedan with spotlights mounted on both sides. I ease in behind them and hit them with my red light and floodlight, and they freeze. But only momentarily. As I step out and approach the vehicle afoot, they accelerate, blasting me with gravel and dirt, leaving me in a fog of dust. I leap into my car to give chase. They are headed south over this dirt road—this road I'm not familiar with—at speeds in excess of seventy, training both spotlights back at me.

Because of the thick dust, the lights, and my unfamiliarity with the road, I hang back, where I have some visibility ahead. The Ford has Colorado plates, and one thing I know for sure: the farther south they go, the farther from Colorado and the closer to the Taos jail they are going to be. Of course, the first lesson here is that I have not learned this road. The second lesson is going to come if I do not catch them soon; I hadn't fueled my car that evening before going home, and the gauge is riding on E.

They turn east at a road intersection. They can now plainly tell that I trail them by a good half-mile, as they can see me coming along behind, approaching from the north. It is obvious that they plan to intersect the main north-south highway, which will take them back to Colorado, home free. And after all, if they outrun me this well over a dirt road, well, just wait till they hit the pavement and open up that V8 Ford.

Maybe. What they do not count on is that I am driving a Dodge Polara police cruiser with a big engine and four-barrel carburetor (a big, gas-eating, four-barrel carburetor, I'm thinking at the time). They reach the highway and head north, still flashing me with their left spotlight, as if to say *Adios, amigo mio*. I hit the pavement and punch it; the four-barrel bellows like a bull, and I have them stopped before the line, fair and square.

Lee is still stuck.

I load the four adults and their three rifles into my car, letting the fifth one, a juvenile, take the Ford on back to Colorado. I head for Taos—and run out of gas four miles down the road. They were that close to being home free in Colorado. It is about two-thirty in the morning, and it is six before we arrive safely at the Taos jail after waking up half the population to get some gas hauled out to me.

I cannot, for the life of me, remember whether it is before or after a big breakfast of ham and eggs that I go back to help Lee out of the ditch.

An old gentleman comes by my house late one evening, during a period when I'm stationed in the eastern New Mexico community of Portales. He says I should know that a particular cafe downtown is using venison in place of beef in the stew. I ask how he knows. He says he wants to keep that part of it confidential, but if I have to know, his sister is a waitress there. Will his sister talk to me? No. Well, a bit of hearsay information like that will not do for probable cause for a search warrant; however, I figure the old man is probably telling the truth, and it sounds challenging.

It can be more frustrating nabbing a wildlife violator, from the investigative aspect, than trying to solve a robbery. For one thing, there's often little cooperation from witnesses or other people who know of the violation. Often it's figured that a poacher hasn't done anything heinous enough for a person to stick their nose into. Occasionally someone will anyway.

The use of uninspected meat for public consumption is a serious violation of the health laws in New Mexico, no less so if that meat is wild game. More importantly to me, I want to know where these people are getting venison this time of year. Deer season has been over for several months.

I call on my friend Nando Mauldin, an officer who is assigned to a neighboring district. Business has been slow, and we both agree we need to stir something up. Nando drives on over and, dressed in his western shirt and Levis, takes my family car on down to the cafe in question to have some lunch.

Sure enough, the special that day is stew. Nando captures a few choice pieces of the meat in his napkin before finishing off his lunch.

Back at the house, we scrutinize, taste, handle, and sniff that meat like a couple of hotel chefs, but cannot for the life of us decide what it is. So we strike up a plan. Later in the afternoon Nando goes back to the cafe for a cup of coffee, seating himself at the counter where he can see back into the kitchen. I go over to an auto dealer's garage across a vacant lot from the back door of the cafe, and from the outside phone booth I call the cafe and ask for the owner. I tell him who I am, that I am downtown, and that I want to stop by to ask some questions about the meat they are using.

The owner says OK. I step out of the phone booth and eyeball the back door of the cafe. Inside, Nando watches a considerable amount of hustle and commotion in the kitchen, and hears anxious voices talking about the game warden coming over. I watch as someone in a white apron stumbles out the back door with a large pot and dumps the contents into the garbage can next to the steps. I jump in the car, drive across the vacant lot to the cafe, and enter the open back door. Nando is already in the kitchen. In a large kettle on the counter are about fifteen pounds of cubed-up meat being readied for suppertime stew. Through an open meat locker door, in plain view, hang two skinned deer and parts of another. I tell the proprietor that that—pointing at the deer—is what I want to talk to him about.

He says quietly, "Yeah, that's what I figured." (One thing about those days, you did not get lied to so much.)

Anyway, they had a fairly good enterprise going, poaching deer at night with a spotlight back up on the Caprock and supplementing the fare on the menu with a little venison.

The judge slaps a pretty harsh fine on them, and the last time I eat there, they are not serving venison in the stew. At least I don't think they are. Sometimes I don't know deer meat when it stares me in the face.

A GAME WARDEN LEARNS to keep his eyes focused on the sides of the roads and trails. It becomes second nature, like a highway patrolman looking at license plates or a city police-man watching for suspicious people around a shopping mall at two in the morning. I notice the cardboard box on the shoulder of the Piños Altos Highway, just outside of Silver City, long before I come abreast of it. I do some fast braking when I see what appears to be a deer hide sticking out of the box. It is indeed a deer hide. There is nothing unusual about it except that it is fresh, and deer season has been closed for some time.

I dump out the hide and examine the inside of the box. Underneath one of the flaps on the bottom is a pay stub, giving the date a couple of years previous, the name of the payee, the company, and the name of the town—somewhere in Illinois, I believe.

I check the Silver City phone book. The name is there.

The man who comes to my knock on the door answers to the name on the stub. I say, "Are you the same Bill Jones who used to work for such-and-such company in Illinois back in 1963?"

"Why, yes . . . why?" he answers, unable to place me, other than he can see I'm a game warden.

"I need to talk to you about the deer."

"Oh," he says, with a defeated look in his eyes, probably deciding that I know the whole story, since I obviously already know the history of his life.

"Well, you had just as well come on in," he says, opening the door wide. "We're just having some of it for lunch."

Maybe if we leave the old bear alone,
he will simply come down from the tree
and leave. It's a good idea, but
it doesn't work.

CHAPTER NINE

Running Charley
Out of Town

I first learn of Charley when Bonito Martinez of Taos calls to say his yard dogs have a large bear up a tree. "You're the game warden," he says, "so maybe you can do something." I tell him I'll be right there.

By 1968 I felt I had tackled about everything in the previous nine years with the Game and Fish Department. That is, most anything having to do with game and fish law enforcement, game surveys, and predator control. But during the next two days these would all take a back seat to being a traffic cop, manipulating fire hoses, and controlling crowds: Charley had come to town.

When I drive into the Martinez farmyard on the outskirts of Taos that Monday afternoon in May, a small crowd is already gathering. As Martinez said, there is a large cottonwood tree, a myriad of dogs yapping around it, and a big black bruin sitting comfortably in the first fork, not more than fifteen feet above the ground. He is a healthy bear, in good form—not old and poor like you might expect of one rummaging for groceries in and about the town limits instead of being up in the hills where he belongs. He sits in the fork of the big cottonwood watching us with unguarded interest as we parade about. Once again, as with the mountain lion of years before, he is more interested in the dogs than in the people.

I suggest to Martinez that he remove the dogs; I will handle the people. Maybe if we leave the bugger alone, he will simply come down from the tree and leave. It's a good idea, I think, but it doesn't have a chance to work. More people wander in from the main road; word is spreading. By late afternoon school is out, and every kid in town shows up with a dog under each arm. It would have taken the militia to discourage the onlookers. These people live at the very edge of bear country, the Sangre De Cristo Mountains, yet a bear in town is a rarity.

Charley is taking it all rather calmly, so I decide to sit back and wait for dark. But well after dusk, headlights continue to find their way down the dirt road to the Martinez farm. By midnight things appear to be in hand. The people have gone home, and the dogs are tied. I am certain that the hullabaloo has dispelled any lure that the garbage cans of Taos might have originally had for Charley, so I leave, hopeful that the morning sun will find him gone back to the hills.

Bright and early Tuesday morning everything is quiet, and by nine I am beginning to admire the wise decisions I have made. Around nine-thirty the phone rings. It is the newspaper calling: Charley is still in Taos. This time I find the big bruin in another, larger cottonwood, still on the Martinez farm, still rather calm. The dogs, no longer tied, have done their deed. This time Charley has climbed higher, to about twenty-five feet above the ground.

It's time to get serious. Charley is bound to become a little irritable at all this, and I have other things to do. I radio for help to my partners, Allen Vickery and Lee Cordova, then go into town and commandeer an REA line truck with a cherry-picker bucket hoist and crew to go with it. By the time I return, Charley has gained another ten feet in elevation. The crowd is gathering again. It's time to move them back and start trying to work the bear down out of the tree from above.

I am hoisted in the cherry-picker bucket to a point a little above Charley and near the same branch he is on—in fact, a bit too near the branch. Rather than being frightened out of the tree, he heads up the branch toward me, clawing, scraping, and popping his teeth. Desiring to appear as cool as possible to the growing audience, I casually ask the bucket operator down below to move me away from the branch. This he doesn't do. Maybe he hasn't heard my casual request. Charley is still coming, so this time I make certain the operator hears my call of distress—but he moves me toward the branch instead of away from it. (Is it possible I've given this guy a ticket sometime in the past?) My third distress call resembles anything but the voice of a fearless controller of predators, but it gets the immediate attention of the operator.

As I am lowered to earth, Charley makes his move . . . up to forty-five feet. Now he is definitely out of reach. The pressure is on. It is plain that Charley is becoming irritable. Lee, Allen, and I go to work. The portable live trap and capture gun are summoned from Santa Fe, with a stopover at Los Alamos to pick up tranquilizing drugs. The Taos Fire Department's new tanker truck is dispatched, and the State

Police are asked to turn traffic back at the main road.

An old adage claims there is a drunk in every crowd. This crowd is no different. Where he comes from, I don't know, but before I know what is happening, this drunk has doffed his shirt, shoes, and socks and is climbing that rough-barked cottonwood with the agility of a spider monkey, mumbling something about "gettin' that ol' bear outta there . . . poor ol' devil." No threats or persuasion I offer will bring the drunk back down. Charley climbs higher. The drunk pursues. Charley is up to sixty feet now, about as high as he can go and still be in the tree, and the drunk is right there with him, try-ing to talk him down. "Come on ol' feller, nobody's gonna hurt you with Uncle Billy here." Charley pops his teeth in answer, and I'm not sure what his next move will be. It is becoming a long day.

I prop the high-caliber rifle along the top of the patrol car for a steady aim. If Charley makes for the drunk, it is going to have to be a killing shot (unfortunately for Charley, not the drunk). Sweat trickles down my back. The humor in all of this is now somewhere in the past. But finally, after running out of conversational material, the drunk begins to retreat. The crowd cheers. I breathe a sigh of relief. Charley stays put.

The help from Santa Fe arrives. The bear will have to be encouraged to a lower elevation due to the inaccuracy of the tranquilizer gun, and because a fall from that height will cer-tainly kill him. It is time for the 800-pound-pressure fire hose. Again I go aloft in the bucket. I blast Charley good with the fire hose, again and again. He loves it. He hasn't had a drink for a while (not that the drunk hasn't offered him one). He positions himself to take best advantage of the torrent of water, and stays where he is. The crowd loves it.

It's no use. Charley will have to be drugged where he is. From the highest point the cherry picker can stretch, Allen Vickery takes aim from his perch in the bucket. The dart strikes home in Charley's butt. He isn't amused, and starts inching down the tree. The drowsier he gets, the farther down the tree he moves. The second dart strikes within a few inches of the first. When the effect of the tranquilizer loosens the bear's grip on the tree, he falls, but by then he is only about twelve feet from the ground. He bounces a little but is unhurt. We manhandle him into the bear-trap trailer as fast as possible as the spectators rush in to get a closer look.

Later, in the Costilla Range of the Sangre De Cristos, forty miles north of Taos and at the far end of an old logging road, Allen and I patiently wait for Charley to wake up inside the trailer. When he is fully awake, we open the door and stand well back. Charley cautiously eases out, looks around, sees us, and makes a dash for the nearest tree. He puts his front feet up on the big ponderosa pine, peering high into the branches, then looks back at us. Then he peers back up into the tree, maybe weighing the likely consequences of his decision, then looks back at Allen and me again, gets down on all fours, and casually walks off, examining oak bushes as he goes. Sore ribs, raw butt, but happy, I figure.

He shot one of the last of the Mexican gray wolves and saw "a fierce green fire dying in her eyes." It haunted him forever.

CHAPTER TEN

Trailing through Leopold's Wilderness

I ride out from the Heart Bar Ranch on the devil-striped dun. It will be two days on patrol: up the Middle Fork of the Gila River, over the top to Prior cabin, then off the rim at Hell's Hole to the West Fork and back. Fifty miles maybe; bedroll and slicker tied aft of the cantle, a few odds and ends in the saddlebags. I ride along the edge of the paved road for a mile or so, then leave that improvement behind for the ridge trails, over the top through juniper and piñon and down into Little Bear Canyon, so narrow that you can almost touch the 200-foot-high sheer rock walls on both sides of the canyon at the same time. It is deep, shadowed, curving serpentine, and almost cavernous; cool, quiet; hooves on wet gravel.

I think about the pavement left behind (it once took all day in a truck over hot boulders just to get back here), and I think of the new National Park and U.S. Forest Service Visitors Center: brick, steel, glass—and employees handing out information to touring souls who probably didn't drive all the way out here to look at glass, brick, and steel.

There are trout here in the Gila Wilderness: rainbow, brown, and cutthroat. Below the junction of the three forks, you can catch channel catfish and smallmouth black bass to boot. No large fish in these ribbons of water, just frying-pan size. Thoreau said, "It is the poetry of fishes which is their chief use; their flesh is their lowest use." Yes, Henry, but even so, you can cut an eighteen-inch brown trout in two sections, salt and pepper, shake in a sack of flour, fry in a bacon-greased iron skillet on cedar coals, throw in your potatoes and onions, slice a tomato, boil some hot, black coffee. There will be time to think of the poetry while presiding over the experience for a moment, valuing the savory tastes and thanking the deity of your choice.

These fish are as wild as any you will know in New Mexico. They are not raised in a hatchery, only hatched there (the browns and rainbows); the rest are indigenous. In the old days, we would pack over half a million fry up the forks each year. On mules. Like this: A hatchery truck would travel all night from up north; milk cans aerated, ice added as needed to maintain constant, cool temperature; 300,000 fry in those twenty cans. Ten pack mules saddled and ready at daylight, fry dumped into pack cans formed to fit a mule's ribs, ice chunks added—fish still happy. Head for the high country, mules strung out at a trot (keeps the water aerated). Stop every few miles, lay two cans in the water to let the temperature merge slowly, tie the mule to a tree, onward with the rest.

The mules love to be turned loose afterward. Tie empty cans on, secure lead rope, turn 'em loose, yahoo! A mule hates for another mule to get ahead of him, so ten mules ratt-ley-bang their empty cans down through the timber. Then the whole bunch sees some good grass and stops to graze. Quietly. When you catch up to them it is once again rattley-bang, kick and fart, hell-bent.

Yahoo.

Some folks look down their noses at mules. A fine mule with a roached mane and trimmed tail is a thing of beauty, though I know beauty is a term with prejudices. But you don't look at a mule with a horse in mind; you look at a mule with a mule in mind.

Water birch, willow, scrub oak, grapevine, sycamore, cottonwood, walnut in the bottoms. Yellow columbines cling to cracks in the rocks, Spanish daggers plume the granite rimrock, and purple Russian thistles stand out in small, hot openings away from the water. Diamondback rattlesnakes: A dog or horse won't usually die of snakebite; these are man-killing serpents, fangs injecting venom into the aching veins. Herman Ogren got bit on his wooden leg; is a man lucky to have a wooden leg, or what?

The dun eats grass: chomp, chomp, chomp. I have dropped the reins so he can forage where he wants. But he wants to eat up near my ear as I lie there. Chomp, chomp. I listen to the sound; is he going to step on me, damn it? The grass sounds very tasty, and I visualize the giant molars grinding away. I hear all the sounds up close. The juices in his paunch, little gurgles. The saddle creaks. Swish, swish, swish, his lips are gathering a big bite of gramma grass. Chomp, chomp, chomp, chomp. A trickle of juices, a rumble from his gut. A whining intestine. He rests, listening for a moment. His big brown eye is moist, thoughtful; the long lash blinks. The dun moves away to some better clump.

Relationships. We associate without words with our

domestic animals. Well, yes, we talk to them, but they comprehend little from the words. They understand meanings better through the eyes, and by the manner in which we convey the words. Sometimes we do not relate this well with people. Usually we are not keyed in to them; we avert the eyes. The eyes speak meanings from the heart. But not with all life. We won't understand a snake through its eyes; we would have to connect some other way. Maybe with its energy—exchange with it. Some people can do that. Perhaps they are on a higher plane, but a natural one.

THIS GILA WILDERNESS was the first of the national wilderness areas established; Aldo Leopold's child, 1924. It was right here—he was a young forest supervisor then—right here in the Gila Forest that he shot one of the last of the Mexican gray wolves and saw "a fierce green fire dying in her eyes." It haunted him forever. He said so. I think it was all right for Aldo to kill that wolf. Maybe it was meant to be. It was better that one of the last of the Southwest's gray wolves be killed by Aldo Leopold than by someone who would not contemplate what he had done.

I AM ABOUT SIX MILES below the meadows. A thunderstorm creeps in over the high bluffs. The muffled thunder has seemed distant. Now it strikes fire in the deep canyon, splits the atmosphere. The devil's dun almost unseats me but settles down after the third crack. Rain immediate. With the lightning

I face a quandary: get under a tree, get out in the open, which? I ride over near some smaller trees; take my chances.

Up on the East Fork I once found three Hereford cows under a tall yellow pine, fried. I ruminate on that. The dun and I, we both sit it out, take it all in: the bolts of lightning, the rain, the splitting, sizzling, burning air explosions piled on us. A tree across the canyon is riveted. Christ! I had a cousin who was killed by lightning, changing a flat tire along the highway. Speak to me, Lord, in kind ways.

THERE IS A SMALL CANYON over on the main river a few miles below the junction of the east and west forks. The mouth is hidden. You ride the trail near the river, and you don't notice that a canyon should be there, it's so overgrown with grapevine and piñon. I wish now I could remember how a friend and I found it back then. We rode back several hundred yards through the brush and trees, and the first thing we saw was a hieroglyph, a large circle stained into the rock wall, with colors of the rainbow in it—a circle with smaller circles inside, like an archer's target—up far enough that we could not reach it.

I climbed along a rock ledge, attempted to stretch and touch the circle. There were meanings there I was not sure of. Emerson said, "Our life is an apprenticeship to the truth that around every circle another can be drawn; that there is no end in nature, but every end is a beginning; that there always is another dawn risen on midnoon, and under every deep a lower deep opens."

I named the canyon Colonel John Franklin Smith, Jr.

Canyon after a friend, the friend who was with me at the time. Frank and I snooped around that canyon mouth and found a cave at ground level with walls built on the front. There were burnt corn cobs and pottery pieces on the floor and a portion of an Indian sandal, in amongst the nesting sticks of a pack rat. Most interesting to me was the handprint in the mud chinking on the wall: a small hand, maybe that of a twelve-year-old, or of an adult of that period. Back in A.D. 1200. Anasazi. They were the cliff dwellers who vanished with no reasons written under the ancient dust. We left it all touched—symbolically for the circle—but left it as we found it.

THE DUN TRAVELS at a comfortable pace, an easy jog of about five miles within an hour along the Middle Fork bottoms. That also allows for the numerous river crossings, one every few hundred yards. Back and forth, the clean water seeks its way from mountain base to mountain base; deep, green holes under strict rock bluffs—cathedrals. Riffles over pebbles, sycamores shading the open stretches, roots feeling their way to the river. Drink the river. The dun drinks, sucking, filling the big tank. I drink, the sky drinks, a trout darts. The earth is alive, a great organism.

BEAR MOORE had been eaten by a grizzly somewhere up around the San Mateos; well, not eaten, but close to it. He came back here to the Gila to continue looking for, and dreaming about, gold. Once he had recuperated, he came back partly for the gold, but mainly to hide his ugly, mauled, misshapen face. The manzanita bushes did not care what Moore looked like. That was in the 1880s. He lived in a cave over on Turkey Creek most of the time—mined over there. But he had several caches around the country. One cabin he built is still there on the West Fork, fallen down, roof long gone, but part of the walls still standing. There are portholes on each side, holes beveled to allow for shooting from any angle. He had a garden, pumpkins and corn, and it may be that that place was as civilized as he got, although it was said that he wrote a diary in a fine, educated hand. James F. Moore, from St. Louis, Missouri.

There were a few folks he would talk to—he visited the store in Piños Altos once a year—but he shunned most people, and just prospected, hunted, and set heavy, intricate, log bear traps all over the country. In the 1920s, a government hunter found old Bear Moore's remains over on the west side of Brushy Mountain a few weeks after a great snowstorm. Bear had some venison in a tree there and a few beans, and there was sign of a campfire, but it looked like the old man had fallen down behind a log and just could not get up. The hunter rode out and got some help. They buried him there in a header canyon under some big ponderosas. Nobody knows where it is now. Bear Moore would like that.

WHEN I REACH THE MEADOWS the rain has softened and has that look of becoming a drizzle, unusual for this country. I am wet from the thunderstorm of two hours before. I have a slicker, a large one covering even the saddle and down to my shins. But it has rained so hard, beaten down so fast and hard, that it has soaked through my hat and run down the sides of my face and neck in streams, soaking my shirt and undershirt through to the waist. My two packets of book matches are pulpy, and I am this way as I ride into the meadows, late. The next time I will bring a box of wooden matches rolled up in cellophane.

The trail to Prior Spring leaves the Middle Fork of the Gila here at the meadows. An hour's high climb up out of the grapevines, oak brush, sycamores, and cottonwoods into the ponderosa, the juniper and mahogany folds along the rim-rock. As the trail zigzags west it is like climbing back into the day from out of the deep canyon shades of evening, this on an ordinary day. But today there is not a late sun to give a feel for the time of day. Cresting out of the canyon I am greeted not by a sinking sun, but by the gray of the drizzle and fog hanging like the leaf smoke of a heavy autumn burn. Lateness just arrives, like that, and earlier than ordinarily.

It is another four or five miles to Prior, an hour, and as dark dims the pines and rocks to blackness, I finally have to give the horse his head; I can't see the trail. I don't want to spend a long night siwashed under a juniper bush within shouting distance of a dry, warm cabin. The night is black, the wet shirt cold. It is time to stop, that's all there is to it. I see an apparition, barely discernible, ahead in the black. Ghostlike, it is almost metallic; it *is* metallic, the tin of the cabin roof at Prior.

That night it rains hard; it wakes me, off and on, beating on the roof. I am warm and dry, tamales and bread digesting properly, dishes done, fire banked in the iron stove, the dun grain-fed in the round corral with head low and eyes closed to the rain, slicker over the saddle on the rail. The resident rats run against the log walls searching out new scraps; tin-can lids nailed over holes in the floor are for decor only. But the rats are no concern to me. I am only glad they have company and that I am not hunched against a bush in the rain of a black night.

THE CABIN HERE belongs to the Game and Fish Department, on a parcel of pieces of private land purchased by the state along with the headquarters of the old Heart Bar Ranch. The old private land here—right here where I lay at Prior Spring—was won by blood and sweat in the late 1800s. In November and December of 1885, while the Chiricahua Apache Geronimo was hiding out down in Mexico, one of his younger followers slipped back across the border to make a name for himself by killing gringo and Indio alike on a rampage covering about twelve hundred miles in less than two months. Fewer than a dozen renegades were with Josanie, but he had several hundred U.S. Cavalry troops from Fort Bayard, Alma, Horse Springs, and Fort Apache combing the country for him. Like swatting hornets' nests with a stick, Josanie made his way through the Gila country and adjoining areas ambushing and killing settlers, soldiers, Navajo scouts, and twenty White Mountain Apaches, mostly women and children, at San Carlos.

With six captured White Mountain Apache women and a child, Josanie lit out for the high country—to this country here where I lie in my bunk—losing his horses and supplies in a skirmish with Lt. Samuel Fountain and his troops from the

Eighth U.S. Cavalry. The next day, December 10, the loose Apaches killed the only non-Indians who had probably ever lived here between the Middle and West forks of the Gila: Thomas C. Prior, John Lilley, and Presley M. Papenoe, a French Canadian trapper; three men carving out their separate niches in the wilderness. After discovering the bodies of Prior and Lilley at the Lilley cabin on Clear Creek, Papenoe was waylaid trying to make it back to his own place near the Middle Fork. Three more men were killed over at Raw Meat, west of the West Fork: the McKenzie brothers from Ireland and William Benton.

Ten days later Josanie ambushed Lieutenant Fountain near Little Dry Creek while the troopers were on their way from the WS Ranch to Silver City, killing five soldiers, including a military surgeon, Dr. T. J. C. Maddox. Finally, after killing some thirty-seven people—he lost only one of his own men—and before escaping safely south into the Sierra Madres of Mexico, Josanie and his little band killed a storekeeper and freighter by the name of Sauborin while the man was on his way from Silver City to the mining settlement of Cooney. They hauled off what they could, including a box of fancy toilet soap, which they found useless after biting into one of the bars, and some little heart candies they also found not to their taste—little hearts that said "I Love You," "Kiss Me," "You Are My Honey," picked up along their trail by Army scout James H. Cook.

BUT HERE AT OLD MAN PRIOR'S SPRING tonight, there are no ghosts of eighty years ago, only the rain, only the rats. I lie here and I think about the time we—the dun and I—left here for the Trotter Place up the Middle Fork. I had a pack mule that time, and a nice pot of pinto beans I had made the day before and hated to throw out; so I packed them, pot and all, in the panniers. It was an all-day trip, at a jog most of the way. Late that night at the Trotter Cabin I set those beans on the stove to heat up. I had been thinking all afternoon about how good they were going to be. I fished a spoon in there, and not a bean was left. All pounded to bean soup.

I REMEMBER, TOO, an earlier time, a December, that Shel Lowrance and I took our saddle horses, along with a couple of pack mules, and headed up the West Fork for White Creek Ranger Station, about twenty-eight miles from the Heart Bar, where some beaver had drawn the complaints of the U.S. Forest Service. The beaver had been cutting large cotton-wood shade trees along the river and damming water back up into the horse pasture. I would take care of the beaver trap-ping; Shel would tend to some game watering units. No one occupied the log cabin ranger station during the winter, so we had the place to ourselves. There was plenty of grain and hay in the barn for the stock, plenty of wood to cut for kindling, and a pressure cooker for beans and stew.

I set traps on some slides and crossings over the dams, while Shel tended the first pot of beans and gathered in some wood. That night it commenced to snow in earnest. By the fourth day it had snowed twenty-three inches with no sign of letting up. I had taken ten adult beaver, skinned and fleshed them, and packed the pelts in snow to maintain their freshness until I could get them home for stretching. It was enough to ebb the population, and we figured we had better vamoose if we wanted to get back to our families by Christmas. But it was not a happy decision. We were comfortable in our wilderness retreat, experiencing what I believe is the primal sensation of tending to basic needs away from civilization. True, the accommodations at White Creek Ranger Station were not rough, but I have felt the same comfort inside a brush lean-to, dry and out of the rain, with a fire blazing and plenty of wood gathered.

At White Creek, Shel and I were at ease with our surroundings and with each other. We knew our individual responsibilities and chores, and best of all, we knew when to respect each other's space. With a partner in the woods, you try to exceed what is expected of you. I have always thought that if you really want to know the value of a partner, take the partner camping.

BACK HERE at Prior cabin, in the morning, the clouds break away, and there is a flare of sun along the pine tops and a blue to the color of the day. Now there is the clean smell of wet yellow pine needles and cedar. I lock up, saddle up, and head for Hell's Hole on the West Fork. I look back at the cabin before the trail bends away: wood smoke trailing from the stovepipe, on a quiet day with a new sun on the wet grass that covers the earth nicely throughout large openings spotted with great yellow and red ponderosas.

I won't see the cabin again for a quarter of a century, but I don't know it then. I just look back because I like seeing it, much the same way you might glance back and admire some-thing that belongs to you just because you never get tired of seeing it. Only this place does not belong to me; it is more like I belong to it. There are many comfortable places in the world, but only a few where you feel like you are home.

"... [N]ow I see the earth as it really is,
never again will I see things as I saw them
yesterday or the day before."

—N. Scott Momaday
The Way to Rainy Mountain

PART THREE

THE BUSH

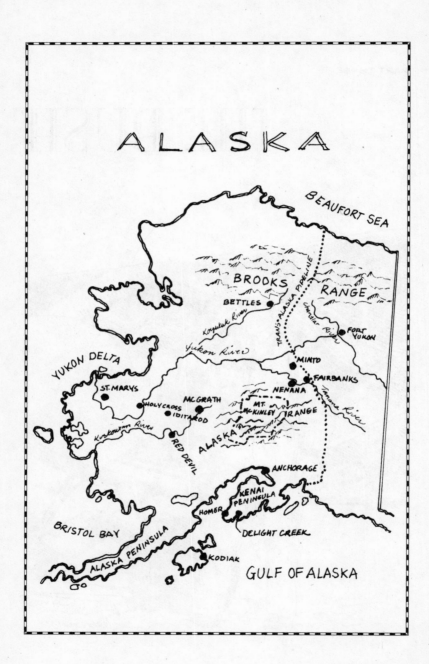

The sound of a Piper Super Cub has a significant meaning to a wolf. It signifies death advancing from the sky.

CHAPTER ELEVEN

The Wolf

I spent ten years with the New Mexico Game and Fish Department. The last year was in a bird cage, the head office in Santa Fe. There was a title with the job, but the freedom was gone: turn the renegade loose in the woods for nine years, then chain him behind a desk. Sack lunch; white shirt and tie. Thirty-one years old and then a desk and four walls for twenty more years. Isn't that gray hair showing in the mirror? Isn't that a grinding in the stomach? The Alaska Department of Fish and Game needs officers. I pick up the phone.

THAT FIRST YEAR IN ALASKA, 1969, we move into the village of Anderson, just north of what was then known as Mt. McKinley National Park, buy a small house, settle in. It is a good place for the kids, with woods and creeks running in all directions from the edge of town. But for me, as a fish and game officer, it's frustrating at first. I'm in a big district full of airplane-driving hunters and guides, with no way to cover it adequately. There is only one road, running north and south. The district has never been assigned a patrol aircraft; I'm the first pilot/officer to be stationed there. But I'm finally assigned an airplane, a Piper Super Cub, sharing it with the Fairbanks district.

That winter there is an illegal wolf-killing operation going on. Edmund Lord has noticed that someone is sharing his trapline area. He finds airplane ski tracks, and footprints leading to a kind of trap-set he hasn't seen before. When he brushes away some of the small pieces of caribou meat surrounding the set, an explosion sends him reeling backward into the snow. He sits there in a stupor, staring back at the device that has violated the winter silence, scaring the living hell out of him, there on the frozen Teklanika River, more than eighty miles from another human soul. He begins to examine himself for injuries. His right glove is torn by the blast, but the skin is barely broken.

Edmund Lord, native son of Alaska, is lucky. The blast is from a cyanide gun, referred to as a "coyote getter" in the West. If the powdered cyanide had entered his bloodstream through an open cut, he would have died. If he had breathed the vapor expelled from the blast, it would have paralyzed his lungs. In six seconds an adult coyote can run a hundred yards. That's as far from a cyanide gun as I ever found one after he had gasped the exploding powder. In other words, as far as he could get with air no longer a factor in his life. That is how quickly Edmund would have died: a matter of seconds—not even enough time to reach his snowmachine seventy-five feet away.

But Edmund did not know what it was that blew up in front of him, even after he dug the gun out of the frozen ground and studied it. It was in a small metal tube driven into the ground, and there was a trigger mechanism screwed onto a hollow, cloth-covered barrel an inch long, smeared with caribou blood. Inside was a spent .38-caliber pistol cartridge. He knew then that it was some kind of set gun, but who the hell would be putting out set guns on his trapline? He gathered up his rifle, stuffed the coyote getter in his coat pocket, and headed for his home in Nenana. He called me when he got there.

As soon as he shows me the getter, I know what it is. These guns were an effective way of killing coyotes in New Mexico. In Alaska they are definitely illegal to use for taking wolves or anything else.

Edmund is already upset about someone moving in on his trapline. When I tell him how close he came to having more than just a bullet through the hand, he becomes angry. "I want this person caught," he says. "One of my kids could've been with me, and maybe this damned thing would've killed him."

"OK, let's talk about everything you've seen out there on the line this past week."

He says he has noticed a red airplane in the area, but never close enough to see the numbers. He says he found once, by their tracks, where the hunters had killed a wolf; not by trapping, but by shooting. At least he thought it was by shooting. When he examined the site where the two people had picked up the wolf along the frozen river, there was no blood, nor sign of blood in the wolf tracks, yet the wolf had been running hard when he died.

"Did you backtrack the wolf?" I ask.

"Not very far," he replies. "But if I had, I would have found one of these set-gun places. Right?"

"Probably," I agree. "Can you show me where the wolf was taken, if we fly out there?"

"You bet."

That afternoon we examine the place where the wolf was taken. The wolf's tracks lead back to the riverbank, where we find a disturbed area in the snow, along with bits of meat and suet. Closer examination produces a cyanide gun. It has been discharged but not reset.

"Who do you know who has a red plane?" I ask Edmund. He names a local big-game guide. I then recall that this guide indeed has a red Super Cub. Things begin to come together. I had received a call only two days before from a friend of the guide, who said he had a wolf to bounty. This would be our wolf.

After dropping Edmund off, I stop by to bounty the wolf. At that time the state is paying a fifty-dollar bounty to encourage eradication of what is considered a nuisance. The man leads me to a shed, where he pulls out the hide of a large gray wolf. There is a yellowish residue surrounding the mouth—a familiar sight to me. Dried saliva mixed with cyanide powder.

I ask him where the carcass is. He says they burned it in the trash dump so it wouldn't attract animals.

Damn.

He says he wants to bounty the wolf for the guide, who has actually taken the animal. He says the guide is not there. I ask him to tell me who was with the guide when the wolf was taken. He names another fellow, so I take the hide and go to see this man. After talking to him, he admits they killed the wolf with a cyanide gun. He says he brought the guns up from Wyoming. He gives me the rest of the guns, about a dozen.

The hide is examined by the State Trooper crime lab. The residue is cyanide. I have my case. Edmund will be pleased.

But not so fast. The law is ruled to have been "improperly promulgated"; therefore, it has not actually been in effect. Sometimes it pays to hire a high-powered defense attorney.

Edmund is not pleased. Neither am I.

I TALKED TO THE NATURALIST at McKinley Park, Dr. Adolph Murie, about the wolf case. He had not heard of cyanide guns in use since the early '50s in Alaska, when the federal government was trying to eradicate the wolves. Now, he said he felt the greatest danger to the wolf in Alaska was posed by the wide-open legalized use of airplanes by hunters and trappers. I soon had to agree.

The sound of a Piper Super Cub has a significant meaning to a wolf—that particular engine chatter differentiated from the drone of any other fixed-wing aircraft or the whopping of a helicopter—the Super Cub signifying death advancing from the sky, like some monstrous mechanical eagle spitting fire and bullets. Wolves do not mistake the sound of the Super Cub, the most common airplane of wolf killers; those ignoring it do not live long.

The age-old castigation of the evil gray wolf had reached the height of effectiveness at that time. The market value for a wolf hide was high, and the state in its wisdom was still forking out fifty bucks per wolf in bounty. Trapping was not the most efficient way to decimate the population. Practically every pilot with a rag airplane and a shotgun was in the air after wolves, and thousands of pellet-ridden hides were being bid on by the fur buyers. Legal hides.

A few bucks bought a trapper's license which entitled the "trapper" to take ten wolves by shotgunning from an airplane in most game units. Enforcing that limit was impossible. The north slope of the Brooks Range lying across the entire breadth of the state—a treeless landscape of rolling hills and measureless plains—was plucked practically clean of arctic grays.

If you are a wolf on the treeless tundra, you do not hide under a dwarf birch; you cannot hide, so you run. And you stop running only when you are dead, or when you lie down in the snow exhausted, awaiting your fate. Or if you are fortunate, you stop when the giant bird has run out of ammo or is short of fuel and finally leaves.

One loner outlaw hunter in particular would take several hundred wolves a year from that country. He bragged about killing entire packs on a single foray. We could not catch him. We did, however, pick up his decapitated body from his wrecked Citabria airplane on the John River one year; his engine mounts had failed him, the errant propeller slicing backward through the windscreen. By then shotguns had been outlawed for taking wolves, and rifles could be used only after landing. His shotgun cartridges picked up at the wreckage were loaded with small-caliber rifle slugs. The chase is a compelling thing.

NOT ALL WOLVES run from people. Some wolves have come to rely on them. During the building of the trans-Alaska pipeline, not too far from Toolik construction camp, a female gray wolf developed a system of stopping trucks along the haul road. She had learned where the sandwiches came from, the ham on rye, peanut butter and jelly, cold beef and mustard. Her plan was simple: lie in the middle of the dusty road awaiting arrival of an eighteen-wheeler, shocking the driver into stopping; advance, then, to the driver's side and stand by for the forthcoming handout. Later, in the summer, after her pups were whelped, she was often seen lying in the road, her pups obediently sitting on the shoulder of the road watching, learning the ropes.

Fourteen years later, I was again working in that arctic area north of the Brooks Range and was not surprised one summer day, fifteen miles north of Toolik Lake, to see a medium-sized wolf sitting along the road waiting for my pickup truck. What generation is she, I wondered, as I pulled up alongside her. Does this old bag have a den full of pups over toward the river? I turned the engine off and sat there talking to her as she looked at me, uninterested, occasionally snapping her jaws at an offending mosquito but seldom taking her eyes off mine. I finally gave up the waiting game and drove on. She remained there, waiting for an easier touch.

I was plagued by the incident. I wondered if we really wanted the wild wolf to become complacent in the presence of man, losing a well-earned fear, and if we wanted wildlife to become hooked on leftovers, handouts, and garbage. Or maybe I simply didn't recognize a "natural" course of events. After all, man and his leftovers are a natural part of things, too. Did I always want wolves to flee when I met them in the wild, or is it a fortunate event to spend a few reflective moments, eyeball to eyeball, thought to thought, with a ferine gray wolf in its natural habitat and with the freedom to leave?

And I further wondered, should we continue to accord unto ourselves the right to decide the ultimate fate of the North American gray wolf?

The wolf deserves better than all the hoopla that has been building to a crescendo for the past twenty-five years or more. My admiration for the wolf didn't vanish, but I became almost ashamed to be identified as even thinking about the animal for fear of being typecast as belonging to one radical side or the other. I realize society polarizes itself on every issue, but I was amazed nevertheless: exalted-wolf-of-mystic-qualities lovers to the left, scorned-wolf-of-game-killing-gluttony haters on the right.

Aboriginal Alaskans, who generally kept outside most of this debate, must have been perplexed by the arguments. They knew the value of the wolf simply for what it is: both a hungry killer of things to eat and a spiritual animal of power. The wolf would no doubt be mystified by even that description. If blessed with reasoning, he would vow contentment in simply being a wolf, happy to be left to his own devices.

Over the years I seldom saw wolves, except while tracking them from the air during winter in order to find their predatory kills for scientific research. I would land to check the remains of the animal killed by the wolves, extracting a sample of its bone marrow to help determine the condition of the animal's health prior to death. It was at those times I learned about the killing nature of wolves, enough to respect the power of jaws capable of breaking open the femur of an adult moose; enough to realize a hungry pack truly utilizes what it kills—hide, bones, viscera, meat—all the way down to just a few big, broken bones left half-drained of marrow and bits of tallow scattered for the ravens and gray jays to pick at.

Although I camped often in wolf country, it wasn't often I'd hear a wolf. The first time was in the fall of my third year in Alaska, about sixty miles up the Nixon Fork of the Takotna River. I was camped in a tent on a gravel bar, lying in my bedroll listening to the drone of an elusive mosquito, when I heard a wolf howl in the distance—a mellow sound, somewhat muted by the fog, coming out of the dim light of late night. The sound was formidable, yet peaceful, signifying the truest form of wildness and wilderness. It was like there was a truth out there you could almost reach out and touch.

In my life I've run the gamut from wanting to kill wolves in defense of what we determine are our rightful possessions, to a personal truce, exalting them to some level of spirituality. But somewhere in the recent past I reverted to thinking of the wolf as I did that night on the Nixon Fork more than twenty years ago: as an animal living its life in the wilderness, and living it best without too much attention.

*Flying is a blood thing. You learn
to fly, and somewhere you overcome
the initial fear.*

CHAPTER TWELVE

In the Clouds

I agree to fly an airplane from Odessa, Texas, to Alaska, for a
friend who has bought it sight-unseen. Here in Odessa it is
ten-thirty, and I've been here all morning waiting for the fog
to lift. A guy is flying the little plane in from a farm or ranch
somewhere. I'm wanting to go. All morning it's been just me
and the airplane owner—I call him Smilin'-Talkin' Jack—in
the cramped office of the hangar; stale cigarette stink, pot of
shallowing coffee made yesterday, thick, like scalded ink,
stenching the air. I wander around outside looking at the
weeds. It is quiet there. I peer into the fog. I think, *With good
luck I'll soon be comfortably situated in the cockpit of the small
plane, heading north, and in a few days I'll be a billion miles north
of this place.*

I hear a Piper Super Cub (you do not mistake those
sounds that have been a part of you for so long). The fog is
burning off and the chattery little plane lands. I check it over
carefully—all is OK.

There is only one thing wrong with this airplane—well,
two things: it has no radio, thus no way to communicate with
control towers and flight service stations along the way for

weather and conditions, and no navigational aids. Texas to Alaska by the seat of your pants.

I get out my charts and draw a line straight through to Lethbridge, Alberta. This gives me a general directional line to wander back and forth on, through mountain passes and via the small towns where I will refuel. Then I take out my sectionals and draw specific direct routes from place to place. This will be thumb-on-the-chart flying all the way, using the telephone when I fuel up to check on the weather ahead and file flight plans. It isn't exactly a daring venture, like Lindbergh crossing the Atlantic, but I feel a kinship with him and with the barnstormers of old. Peaceful flight, low altitude, close to things discernible; wave at the farmer in the field, read the name of the small town on its water tank, land on the back roads for a break.

The West Texas plains—*El Llano Estacado.* The day turns to blue and white. Bright. I dogleg up through New Mexico, familiar terrain to the sand in my veins. The Pecos River: mudhole of a creek when compared to rivers almost anywhere else, but it must have been a sight for parched eyes in those old days of wagon tracks and thirsty mules. Up the east bank; drop in on a familiar ranch road south of nowhere; stretch, relieve. Ol' Billy's haunts, this country; buried just north of here under a gray tombstone chipped by tourists and surrounded by thorny mesquite brush, white sand, and creosote. Howdy, Kid.

IN THE AIR, north into the Sangre De Cristo foothills. To the west, Santa Fe; I learned to fly there. It was there I felt the fear.

Flight:
we transcend to that unknown;
a dimension unexplainable by
language, written or spoken;
suspended,
beyond the beyond.

I remember: I am alone in the practice area, three thousand feet above the ground. I pull the power back while raising the nose; try to maintain altitude. Higher with the nose. The airplane does not like it—it shudders a warning—the stall-warning buzzer screams louder. The controls feel mushy in my left hand, no response; the nose begins to dip, to break. I catch it by lowering the nose, shoving in power. Recovery.

Practice stalls; learn to recover, over and over. Try a few power-on stalls; raise the nose, apply power, raise it further, full power, standing on the tail, shudder, shudder, shudder; BREAK to the right! Drop the nose, catch it. OK, do it again.

There's something I am not liking about all this. In fact, why am I paying good money for airplane rental to tease my mortal fear? It is a fear that has just developed. I am afraid of the airplane now. I fly back to the airport, land, taxi, park, tie it down, call my instructor: "Dick, I don't think I want to continue with this."

"Why?"

We meet for coffee.

"All of a sudden I just got scared up there, Dick. It's the stalls. I think, what if I don't recover? You know . . . what if I get into a spin and don't recover?"

Dick does not talk about it. He says, "C'mon." We go out to the airport, rent a plane, fly out to the practice area. I've

114

never been in a spin. The FAA does not require spin instruc-
tion. Too bad. Dick puts it in a spin—like a revolving single-
leafed seed, downward. Two revolutions; recovery.

"Now, you do it."

I am excited, laughing; nervous, like when you were a kid
and your dad was running along with you while you were trying to ride a bicycle for the first time . . . and then you realize
you are balanced by yourself.

The airplane does not want to spin, it wants to fly; you
have to make it spin. Power off; nose up, higher; shuddering
stall; controls full back; full left aileron, full right rudder—
total cross-control—it breaks over and spins. I am pointed
toward the revolving earth. Hold it in full cross-control to
keep it in the spin; once around, twice around; neutralize
controls (relax); neutralize rudders; add power; recover. The
plane flies.

Climb back up, do it again, lined out along a highway for
reference. This time do one and a half spins; end up going the
other direction; precision. Go back up, do it again; this time
two and a half revolutions. Precision. Back up; three full
spins. We are having fun above the high Santa Fe desert,
Dick and I. My fear of the unknown is gone. I now know the
sensation of, the configuration of, the ultimate result of the
stall/spin. I am balanced by myself.

Flying is a blood thing. You learn to fly, and somewhere
you overcome the initial fear; then it's a have-to thing. Not a
lot else matters. It becomes the love of your life. If you're not
flying, you're down at the airport jawing or hangar-flying,
and looking at airplanes, caressing the lines and outlines, and
whiffing av-gas. If you're not flying, you're there on the tar-
mac alone, like an old tar without a ship, looking out to sea.

INTO COLORADO and back on track. I overnight where I can, where darkness will overtake me, where planning dictates. We Alaska pilots do not think of the Lower 48 as a place to get into trouble, just a place on the charts full of roads and railroads. But on the second day—an afternoon of transition from mid-Wyoming to mid-Montana—I do something that makes me feel dumb.

The weather in Lewistown looks to be good, a little rain shower stuff, broken clouds. I will end up there just before dark. But during the three-and-a-half-hour flight the weather changes a bit, and I see that the mountains clumped up ahead look blue-black with rain. With it getting late, I can be stupid and push through anyway, or just be dumb and circumvent the mountains by following the roads and railroads for better reference, most likely placing me into Lewistown after dark and low on fuel.

I intersect the railroad near Ryegate and turn west with it to Harlowton, where the low, ragged clouds and rain drive me down to a few hundred feet over the town, almost too low to tell which is the main road heading north. But I find it and head north through Judith Gap. I am experimenting right now, wondering if I can see better through the rain and darkness with my prescription sunglasses or without glasses at all; my clear glasses are back out of reach behind the rear seat. I need the light on in the cockpit to follow the chart, but I need it off to clearly follow the wet pavement, shiny with auto headlights. If very worst comes to very worst, I'll try landing on the pavement, provided there are no power lines; at least that is better than a dark mountainside.

Through the Gap country with white knuckles. I think: *Someday I'll come back and fly this route in the daylight, and it will scare me even worse—will scare me to see with clear glasses what I flew by, around, over, and through while in the black night rain with my shades on.*

I turn east at the road intersection west of Lewistown. An airport light will be there somewhere soon, soon, soon. Yes! The relief has to be at least as profound as seeing the lights of Paris, France, in 1927. Fear knows no boundaries; it flows equally into the pulses of heroes and blind game wardens. I splash through the black puddles of a rain-soaked runway. I think about the dangers of flying. Someone called it "hours and hours of boredom, with a few moments of sheer terror." That someone has been there. That night—later that night— it feels good to be safe in the feathers, out of the clouds.

From Montana and on into Canada, I bypass the big airports: Great Falls, Lethbridge, Calgary, Edmonton. I land at the uncontrolled ones: Cutbank, Red Deer, Whitecourt. Now the wilderness of western Alberta—this is more like it! I follow the winding rivers, outlines of distant peaks and ridges, shapes of lakes below. New experience for the little red Cub, but she's grinding along, doing the best she can with no electronics and a magnetic compass that reads thirty degrees off course on good days. We follow the flight routes, imaginary paths, thumb on the chart, and leave the winding, dusty, doglegging Alcan Highway to the truckers and tourists.

My second trip north had been made by driving that highway. It took about nine days just to drive the eleven hundred miles of dirt road through here. Wife, four kids, two cats, rocking chair, saddle, Ford sedan with U-Haul trailer.

I think that drive up the Alcan was not so unlike the experience of my great-grandparents in their 1885 trek from West Virginia to Oklahoma: big mule-powered schooner built by creative hands; white oak timber slung underneath for wheel repairs; ten kids. Stop at a creek once a week, break out the tubs, scrub clothes and bodies. West, west; break sod on the wind-exhausted plains; build a house, a home, a life. Those children grew up and left; drifted away, like awns of wild grass carried on a fall wind—all of them—my father's father's generation (the kids in the wagon). I reflect that I don't know where that forgotten place is, exactly. Buried under fencerows and the reclaiming prairie grass somewhere in southcentral Oklahoma, I imagine.

Of four days in the cockpit, these last two are the longest: twelve hours on the tachometer for each. Good weather, big sky, big country, as I fly north, north, and west, west— Anchorage is as far west as Honolulu—over the boreal forests and deep rivers draining to the north. Four thousand miles the other side of the weeds along the Odessa airstrip.

The little red Cub floats above the endless forest as if suspended on a stationary string. Time is space, it does not move; there is no past, no future, only here and now.

The flat-bottomed riverboats line the silt bank like rafts of basking alligators along a Louisiana bayou.

CHAPTER THIRTEEN

On the River:
Thank Ol' Father John

It's the pre-oil-money days in Alaska. We game wardens don't have a lot of equipment. What we have is good, but we don't have much, and we must share it with other districts. Not having an airplane all of the time, I need to figure out other ways to cover the country. I don't have a riverboat, and there are many miles of navigable rivers that have never seen a game warden closer than two thousand feet above the treetops.

The local Episcopal priest, Father John Phillips, is a friend. He lives in the Tanana River village of Nenana, the major jumping-off port for Interior Alaska villages along the Tanana and Yukon rivers. Alaska's only inland railroad crosses the river at Nenana, where the old sternwheelers that once traveled the Tanana have been replaced by diesel-powered tugs. The major barge line is in Nenana. If you live in Nenana and you work for money, you probably work for the Yutana Barge Line. Or the Alaska Railroad.

If you are a kid, you probably aspire to being a barge line riverboat captain or an engineer on the train. You don't think about having a car—at least not back then. You think about having a riverboat of your own. It will be maybe twenty-four feet long, narrow, of sturdy timbered plywood and two-by-fours, with a lift for raising the motor while you skim over shallow bars. You will build the boat yourself, under the tutelage of an old-timer, and you will purchase the materials and motor with firefighting money. In Nenana the flat-bottomed riverboats line the silt bank like rafts of basking alligators along a Louisiana bayou.

Father John owns one of these boats, and we strike a deal. He will loan me his boat and motor two or three days at a time; we will give him a barrel of gas in trade. It gets me out onto the river. What I learn on the river, reading the water, will be of value when I start flying airplanes with floats. Winding, swirling, drift-infested, muddy river; bobbing widow-makers just beneath the surface, anchored trees ready to spear an unsuspecting hull. Watch for the big boils; they're OK, that's where the water's deepest. Read where the big water volume is likely to flow, cutbank to cutbank. Cutbanks: where spruce tree sweepers lie horizontal, slapping the current.

I like the story told by a guy named Leroy. They spot a humongous hornets' nest on the end of a bushy sweeper, he and a friend. This is the plan: We'll rip by that nest full speed, take one of the oars and wallop that sucker—ha, ha, them little bastards'll be madder'n . . . well, madder'n wet hornets, ha, ha, ha. They do that. Leroy rips by there at twenty miles an hour, the friend clobbers the nest, whap! But the big nest lands in the bow of the boat. Ha, ha, ha. Thirty million screaming hornets. They run the boat up on the bank, abandon it to the winners, and almost don't live through it. It is years before Leroy can talk about it and even crack a smile.

THE STATE TROOPER AND I use Father John's boat to get to the village of New Minto, where they're building the first road into that country from Fairbanks. The people will need licenses before they can drive the road. Nobody has a driver's license. They've been sent manuals to study. When we get there, Lyle is smart: he will give the written tests, safely seated on the steps of the community center, and I'll give the driving tests.

There is a surplus military truck at the village, an old four-by-four left by the government housing construction crew. The people have been practicing. But the truck has no brakes. We simulate driving city streets. Keep it in compound gear; that way you just let off on the gas to stop, then catch the dying engine with the clutch. Pretend there's an intersection here with a stop sign, and you want to turn left. Pretend there are stoplights. All of this on a muddy trail through the village; people getting their driver's licenses, sixteen to sixty-five. Fairbanks, do we have some surprises coming your way!

There is a Fish and Game cabin in the Minto Lakes area, not far from the village. We retreat to there at the end of a day, with a little pike fishing on the way. These northern pike throughout the flatland of the Minto Lakes grow to three and four feet. We don't catch any like that, but it charges the blood just knowing they are there.

Fall time on the Minto. Birch-blazed forest of saffron and burnt sienna. Duck hunters from Fairbanks descend by the floatplane load, pick up their cached riverboats, and charge around the bends, hell-bent, blasting through fleeing waterfowl, shotguns blazing. Game warden sitting there with ticket book. Surprise! Take your ticket like a man; thank ol' Father John, amen.

THE FIRST WHITE MEN trickled, then crowded their way into this Tanana country searching for gold after the big Klondike discovery in '96, searching for the next big strike. They found it here in December 1902; the word was brought out to Dawson City by Jujiro Wada, a Japanese citizen. Seventy years later we pull up alongside a salmon processing vessel in Bristol Bay. It flies the flag of the Rising Sun. A crewman comes aboard our boat. "Wada, Wada," he says. Can he be asking about his countryman from 1902? Finally we figure it out. They need fresh water.

At Tolchakat Slough, an old cabin lies abandoned. Lyle and I look it over with special interest. There's a story here, maybe even a ghost. The man who built it and lived here was paranoid. He rigged a set gun—a shotgun—aimed at the door while he was away. Any intruder who opens that door, Blam! One day he came home. Forgot it was there. That's the story anyway. I believe it. There are pellets still in the doorjamb.

IF YOU SMELL BAD, get out on the river and blow away the stink, they say. Well, I don't know about that, but you can sure blow away the mosquitoes. Of course the biting little devils will get you sooner or later because you have to come to shore sometime. I always dope up before pulling into the bank. You only jump ashore and try to tie up a boat once, without doping up first, to know what I mean.

There are treed islands on this big river, and channels you never see unless you search them out, but a channel might be narrow and end at a sweeper or shallow bar. So you stick with the best guesses—stay with the deep water, hold with the boils and the cutbanks.

You think there may be great, grassy meadows up beyond the riverbanks, places of sweet cleanness, but there aren't. The ground there is silt; gristed grains of a once river among the ferns and willow and white spruce. Sand, you might call it, but it's finer than that, and there's a humidity in there that fastens itself to you. The bugs are bad—mosquitoes, black gnats, and whitesocks that whine and bite—and salt sweat stings the eyes. It is a place to escape from, a strangulation, like the dusty, salt-cedar thicket of a desert. You want to burst out of there, back to the open, blowing coolness of the river.

Up in the flats: river tug coming down, and from the surface you can see that it lies low upon the river, shoving a bulge of smooth water ahead of the barge. In our skiff we turn to catch the wave, trailing like a whale's wake, bleeding away in wide traces toward a caving shore.

PEOPLE DROWN on the Tanana. Lyle and I are always looking for them. Sometimes the bodies are not recovered; the fine silt sand saturates the clothing into great heaviness—tons of it rolling down the river each day. Once we investigate a suicide drowning. You can see the tracks plain in the spongy, damp, muddy sediment along the water's edge. She stacked her clothes neatly, all of them. Barefoot little prints lead straight into the twilight water. Her husband says they had an argument; she said he doesn't love her anymore. He does, but he can't tell her that now.

We have another drowning on the Nenana, a tributary to the Tanana. A young woman—a summer employee at the Mt. McKinley Park Hotel, on vacation from college—falls into a side creek at the park while crossing a wet log. Her boyfriend helplessly watches her being carried away into the big river of glacier melt, her frightened eyes seared into his memory. We search without luck. Forty-five days later and forty miles downstream, kayakers report a body on a sandbar. Lyle goes out to get her, slips her into a body bag, and slings it underneath the helicopter. When he gets back to the airstrip near Anderson Village, the bag is gone. We search for days. Where, across ten miles of green forest, is this green body bag? The search is called off.

A month later the governor orders the search resumed. Pressure from the young lady's home state of Kentucky. There is now five inches of new snow on top of everything, but Lyle goes anyway. He takes the chopper and another trooper, goes out to where he originally found her, then starts back. From the air they see a trace of blood on the snow where a fox has killed a rabbit; they land to look—but really just to get rid of some coffee. They stand around in the snow and discuss what they should be looking for. The other trooper says, "Well, it'll just be a mound in the snow, like this"—and he walks over and kicks a nearby mound. Underneath the snow is the body bag, intact.

I KNEW I WOULD MISS the Tanana country when I got orders to transfer to McGrath later that summer. A country and its people can grow on you. An old trapper friend, Charley Smith, in his sage manner and methodical sense of awareness, kept track of the doings up and down the river. Of the young woman who drowned at McKinley, and the difficulty in finding and refinding her body, he said, "Maybe she doesn't want to go." Can you remove her body from the land while the soul refuses to follow?

Charley Smith, you old Dall sheep poacher, where did you go? You old half-breed British/Athabaskan, solitary woods wanderer, child of the Yukon's Fort Gibbon, raised by the hard nuns of the Tanana orphanage for Indian kids. Where did you go, you old dog-sled lynx trapper, you philosopher and mentor for us young woodsmen—native and interloper alike—you who only trapped enough to replenish your meager larder, refusing to take a single lynx beyond your needs, though the price for pelts was out of sight. Charley, you silent man; you who quietly prophesied that sled dogs "won't run out of gas," but didn't refuse us the privilege of breaking trail with our "iron dogs" when the going got tough and you were too old to be too proud.

Did you think I didn't recognize your gentleness, you who epitomized how man could merge into his environment and supplement the beauty with his presence? I love the thought of your image, Charley. Edmund called me when you were dying, said "Charley wants to see his old friend. When can you come?" Can you forgive my youthful thoughtlessness—my grand rise up the ladder, my tight schedule, a schedule too busy for old friends? Where did you go, Charley? Are you still on the Tanana, and will we see the likes of you again?

One fall, Deacon shot and killed his worthless son-in-law. Deacon said he thought the man was a black bear.

CHAPTER FOURTEEN

Along the Kuskokwim and Yukon

McGrath is a big village on a bend of the muddy Kuskokwim River, across from where the clearwater Takotna River flows in. It is a busy village, centered around its main industry, flying, with the main street part of the airport taxiway. We get settled in. Once again, the woods butt up against town and provide a playground for the kids. A twenty-foot riverboat suffices for Sunday drives and picnic excursions. In the summer and winter I often park the patrol plane on the river which fronts the two-story log house we live in.

I'm the only law enforcement officer for McGrath and several surrounding villages. There is no one else to shove the dirty work off to. Even though we Fish and Game officers have not yet been transferred to the State Troopers, we are still expected to perform as peace officers; in Alaska there are not enough police officers to cover the bush country.

A LITTLE AFTER MIDNIGHT the phone rings. I get out of bed, go downstairs to answer it. "There's a drunk down here at the bar . . . causin' trouble . . . won't leave."

"Which bar?"

"McGuires. Keeps pickin' fights."

"Tell him to go home. Tell him if he doesn't, I'll be down to arrest him."

There are no arguments here with the county, the city, the state, or the feds about who is going to handle what. There isn't anyone else; I will handle it.

One-thirty A.M. the phone rings. "There's a fight down here at McGuires."

"I'll be right there."

Get dressed, bundle up, walk the frozen snow down to the bar. The old beater pickup is buried under four feet of snow, and it's too cold to get the snowmachine started. Hope the fight's over before I get to McGuires because there's nobody to back me up. There's no jail this side of Anchorage, two hundred and fifty miles away by air. If you arrest someone, you put him out in the tool shed, handcuff him to a support bar, light the stove, and hire a citizen as a guard to make sure the prisoner doesn't get hurt or, at fifty below, that the stove doesn't go out. But the fight's over and the fighters are gone; broken pool cue, a little blood. We'll see if someone wants to file a complaint in the morning.

Break-ins, assaults, deaths, drunks, bar fights, family squabbles, property damage, child abuse, drugs, search and rescue, rapes—there's no escape. If you're off in some distant range of the district investigating something else, you have not escaped it; it will be there for you when you get back.

BANGING ON THE DOOR at three A.M. "My neighbor busted out my porch light. Said it was botherin' him!"

"Here's a quarter. Go buy another one. Don't come over here waking me up for this kind of bullshit."

The previous officer here, Jack Allen, said he got tired of answering the door in the wee hours. He let 'em bang away, and if they didn't leave after a while, he answered it. One twilight morning at four there is banging at Jack's door. The banger leaves a little past the cutoff point. Jack thinks, *What the hell, maybe it's important;* goes downstairs, opens the door. A guy is walking off down the road. "Whatta ya want?" Jack shouts.

"Thought you might want to know your airplane's floatin' down the river."

It gets Jack's attention. Running out to the river in his underwear he can just see the floatplane disappearing around a far bend. He grabs the boat and gives chase, still in his underwear. He is lucky. The little Cub hasn't dug a wing into the bank or hit a sweeper. Chugging in the airplane back up the river, towing the boat behind, four in the morning, swatting mosquitoes off bare legs, he thinks, *Someday I could write a book about all this, but I'd have to call it fiction.*

IN THE SUMMER I have to leave the upper villages to handle their own problems. Most of my days are spent on the lower Kuskokwim and Yukon rivers patrolling the commercial salmon fisheries. It is a river fishery. Hundreds of one- and two-man skiffs drifting for king salmon; seven or eight fishing districts opening and closing at different times. I use a Cessna 180 on floats, flying eight and ten hours a day, fueling from five-gallon tins, eating out of a paper sack, sleeping some-times in the plane—tied to the riverbank or on a quiet lake—and sometimes in a shack or tent. If I'm lucky, I stay overnight at the St. Marys Catholic Mission on the Andreafsky River, just off the Yukon. Good food, thoughtful people.

The old nuns at St. Marys would think it scandalous not to be in habit, and they look better that way anyway; they are more streamlined and dignified. They are old nuns—over eighty, over ninety—looking somewhat swallowed up, but lovely in their sanctity. I bring them fresh Yukon kings and they are happy, these old sisters—there in the lower villages since the days when they were bright-eyed girls fresh out of a faraway place.

I was at St. Marys Mission when the pope died—we heard the news on the radio—but I noticed no more reaction than if I was among Baptists down at the drugstore on Main Street, USA, though maybe I'm not Catholic enough to understand. But the response was ordinary, like maybe the pope moved to St. Louis, Missouri, or something.

THROUGHOUT THIS COUNTRY the Yukon is wide, often

more than a mile. And if you fly, you see distinct bluffs from afar and know the river lies there, the bluffs and hills always north of the river. From one bluff to another may be forty or fifty miles across the flats, with the river wandering where it damn well wants to, but always meeting you again at the next bluff. And then beyond, there's always another bluff. . . .

Enter, in the heat of midday, Holy Cross, a large Athabaskan village, silent to the last dog, and know that the people and the dogs must be dead. But no, it is midday; midnight will be different, a time to live. Time to fire up a tune or a three-wheeler. Kids shout all night out in the streets. Booze in town (a flight came in today). Here's to you as good as you are; weep me a tune on the gitfiddle of broken strings. Gang-bang rape, they tell me; woman drunk, too; they all did it to her, even the old man, ninety-two: "Yes, I think he did!" she says. The old man says, "Hell, if I'd of done it she'd know for sure!" She weeps with drunken eyes. That booze no goddamn good for this place! Young guys stole a three-wheeler from the priest. He did not radio for the cops to fly in; he found out who did it—kicked some butt. They didn't do it again.

Out on the river the fishwheels thrum in ceaseless, ancient currents, now and then snatching a silver fish, threading it flopping into the catch box. From the fishwheels comes the chirp of heavy wood on heavy wood.

SOMETIMES I STAY at the site of an abandoned village near the big bend of the Yukon, back behind the bluffs. It is called Ohogamiut, a place no longer a place, but in the high grass against the hill, a frayed Russian Orthodox church stands alone. Here, the site of an old village under the grass somewhere. One old cabin is still there below the church, standing with four walls and a partial roof, and if you lack shelter, the cabin is a good place, but airy and damp, with bugs in thunderous herds. The smoldering Buhach powder helps.

You could stay in the unlocked church. There is a small bell there, cast in honor of that place and dated seventeen-something, and old Russian books, and all the trappings—the whole of it needing in some musty pleasure to be alone. But you wouldn't be comfortable there. You couldn't spit or pass gas. You would stay instead in the fallen-down log place where Old Glory is rolled on its staff, leaning in a dry corner. It is a manufactured flag, with thirteen stars in a circle, but in a different configuration than the one Betsy Ross designed. Old. When I see the flag, I leave it there, but I'm sorry later. I think, *Why didn't I keep that flag?* Eight years later I'm flying on floats in that area and make a special stop. The roof has fallen in, but against the wall, protected by fallen timbers, the flag is still there. I am happy about that.

And I leave it once again.

HERE, IN MUCH OF THIS Oregon-size district where I work, there is no one else to check on the welfare of lone residents, those who are divorced from the villages, who prefer the solitude and independence of life away from some of the strife. Sometimes I pick up the mail for whomever lives along my planned route of patrol, or pick up a needed mechanical part for someone. Old Deacon Deaphon tells me, over coffee at his cabin above Devil's Elbow on the Kuskokwim, "This radio don't talk no more." I have it fixed for him the next time I am in town.

Occasionally I bring fresh fruit to Deacon and Agnes, who goes about the household chores in a homemade wheelchair. She says, "We glad like hell you come!" There is a pleasure in the voice; it keeps me coming back. They are Athabaskans, he in his eighties, she probably ten years younger. I'm told Agnes is one of the last to know the art of making fish nets from animal sinew. She says she is the daughter of "Nushagak Man," whom she never saw—he died back in the '30s—but whom she knew to be the wild man who roamed the mountains of the upper Holitna and Nushagak watersheds in the old days.

Old Deacon, although elderly and sore-footed, stands straight. He is several inches taller than the average Athabaskan, and still barrel-chested. He does not live near any of the villages and is, I believe, a free spirit, living solely off the land, with dignity. He and Agnes raised several children. Most of them lived to adulthood, all but one daughter then dying violent deaths up and down the river. They are buried on the hill behind the house, those that the river or a fire or some other kind of accident might have given up.

When their last and youngest son, an adult of thirty-some by then, was killed in a local snowmachine accident, the river was breaking up and running heavy ice; I couldn't land to tell them, so I dropped a note explaining the circumstances (fortunately, an older grandchild was there who could read). They were asked to meet the plane at a large snow-covered gravel bar upriver the next day, for delivery of the body. Some weeks later a Deaphon granddaughter stopped by my office in

McGrath and presented me with a gift from her grandparents. It was a child's fur marten hat, carefully made, and addressed to my youngest son.

One fall before I knew him, Deacon shot and killed his son-in-law. They were hunting moose together, and Deacon said he thought the man was a black bear. It was well known that the son-in-law was a worthless, wife-beating, child-abusing drunk. Deacon had spent his entire life in the wilds. It is my opinion that on that particular day, the hunting season was open for worthless sons-in-law.

FREE SPIRIT. Most of the settlers and lifelong residents I met in the backcountry had it. And most had stories of interest in their past, whether it was Sam Wright—who had taken a sabbatical from his professorship of theology at Stanford to follow Bob Marshall's trail through the Brooks Range, liked what he saw, and never went back—or eighty-five-year-old Carl Susui, an Athabaskan Indian from the village of Telida, who saw the first white men to enter the upper Kuskokwim country.

A few years before he died, Carl, who was the son of an old Athabaskan chief, told me about those first white men. They were soldiers on an expedition into the Interior from the sea, before the turn of the century. He said that he and his father were in a canoe one day in late fall, hunting moose downstream from the village. They saw a dead horse along the riverbank, and Carl asked his father what sort of animal it was. His father said it was a "white man's dog." They killed a black bear the next day near that area, and its stomach contained a large amount of bacon, yet undigested. They backtracked the bear for most of the day to see where the bacon had come from and finally trailed it into the soldiers' camp.

Carl said the weather had been turning cold, with some snow on the ground. He said the eight white men were suffering and appeared lost. He and his father led them to the village, where they stayed the winter. His mother made them parkas, mittens, and moosehide boots. In the spring his father led the men across the hills to Lake Minchumina and showed them the trail to Fort Gibbon (now the village of Tanana), on the Yukon River. Carl said his family never received any recognition from the government for their help.

ON THE LOWER YUKON RIVER, the delta villages lie split along the mud banks. The houses all face the river channel, which cuts through the center of the villages like a thoroughfare—U.S. Highway 160 through Cherokee, Kansas, maybe, although the flatness and the sameness and the grayness is not broken by section-line county roads or wire fencerows. Here, with dirty glass windows, the houses sit unblinking, as though wide-eyed in curiosity, watching the brown water move thickly on its way to a pallid sea—a sea that hides somewhere to the west, the river having to feel its way with probing fingers to find it.

You could not find the sea yourself without knowing which river channels to follow, because as far as you can see, even on a clear day, there are only thin, flat, rulered lines of horizon where near meets far in the sameness, the grayness, the flatness. Though much of this broad, muddy delta is called land, and some think they own it, great areas are underwater at high tide. Out where sea and river become one or the other, there is only brown water, where maybe you can see a camp on stilts poking up in the middle of nowhere, with some guy sitting on the steps drinking a beer.

The villages with their trash-covered banks straddle the sloughs which are veins of the big river and serve as off-ramps from the watery Yukon freeway for the flat-bottomed skiffs and floatplanes. No one seems to care that the banks are loaded with boat hulls, sunken houses, wringer washers, kicker motors, oil drums, trash heaps, and dog carcasses. What the hell, the junk might help stop the erosion, you see, and out here you want to stop the natural erosion because if you don't, the grinding river will carry you and your possessions off into the Bering Sea.

The wind out here does not know east from west, but blows around the compass, one way or another, always. You are glad it does in the summer, because the bugs would kill you if it didn't. But in the winter? Why does the wind have to blow in the winter, enough to freeze the nuts off a D-9 bull-dozer. The wind serves no purpose then—there are no bugs or stink to blow away—and it kills you with the chill.

Later, in the spring, clouds of birds arrive—waterbirds up from other continents to carry on life's continuum in the ever-yellow grass that fights the flat wind. Cranes, geese, ducks, shorebirds, and cotton-necked tundra swans; rafts and flights, swarms of broken V's, a frontal system of waterfowl, with the noise of spring like distant shouting. You can see the birds there just as they were ten thousand years ago; and the people, too, striking the first meat of spring and burying eggs to ripen mellow.

IN THE SUMMER, it's up the river to fish camp, and Yup'ik families in white canvas tents along the willow banks make smoker fires and mend nets for the king salmon drifts. Pilot bread and canned butter and strawberry jam taste like you remember, and boiled coffee on a gasoline stove and cut fish drying in the perfume of a red-willow smoke are aromas of something you knew before.

The great, brown, moving water sounds like sifting sand, which it is, and along the bank, fish are running beneath the surface, but you can't see them. The current boils out where it's deep. A kicker motor whines like a mosquito, a constant throb, like a skiff circling empty, and I don't care if you can swim, the river silt would weight you down and smother your lungs with the brown water you love.

Up the Innoko fork is old Iditarod; auriferous hills there, wanting to remain silent; creeks asking anonymity lest they fall to the grind of the gold dredge, that bloated barge abandoning boulders in the wake of its torment. And in this old gold camp, there are chalky board buildings too stark even for ghosts, but still remembering young girls who came all the way from Crooked Creek on the Kuskokwim, just to dance. But for someone who knows, it's like they never left, because the silence in the camp and the steep wind down between the buildings say it cannot be so lonely as this; and the mind seeks visions just to keep the soul from dying. Girls dancing in the night.

Jim Fleming was there when I last saw the place. He gave me an old gooseneck coffee pot, one a grizzly had gripped with its teeth. Jim was moving farther back into the mountains. "Too many people around," he said. But there wasn't anyone else, just sounds of creekwater running. And echoes of dancing girls.

One look at all this confirms my
suspicions. These people are bushy.

CHAPTER FIFTEEN

Cold Camp
on the Chandalar

From my Cessna 180 patrol plane I see a lone figure standing in an easy manner out on a gravel bar, looking up. A malamute sits ten feet to the side and watches me in the same way—with mild curiosity. Blue cabin smoke wafts out of a stand of white spruce and threads its way through bright, arctic birch and across the autumn-red willows that grow along the Middle Fork of the Chandalar River. It is a clear-running stream this far into the hills. I'm tempted to land and get acquainted, have a cup of coffee, as I often do when I see someone new in this wilderness. But the Cessna is still on floats, and the river this far upstream is shallow and rocky, too much so to risk damaging the aluminum pontoons for a casual visit.

As a wildlife protection officer, this country, the Brooks Range, is a part of my new assignment in the late '70s. Stretched across the breadth of northern Alaska, the range lies entirely above the Arctic Circle, but it is not desolate or treeless. The south drainages of copious rivers and streams are spread with white and black spruce, red willow and birch; yet the slopes of the steep mountains are open spans of Dall sheep habitat—alpine grasses and lichens and dwarfed arctic shrubs. The mass of the mountains themselves, the ridges, the smaller ranges within ranges, the watersheds overlapping and curling, are an entangled asymmetrical maze, a jungle of alps you cannot see beyond. It is the definition of wilderness. From the spine of the range north, it is treeless, but the north slope has a character of its own, stretching away for over a hundred miles to the Beaufort Sea coast, the whole of it horizonless white in winter. Where does the land end, where does the sea begin?

I had first become mesmerized by the Brooks Range in the '60s when I was temporarily assigned there by the Alaska Department of Fish and Game for aircraft patrol of spring bear and fall sheep hunting. The trans-Alaska pipeline had not yet been built, and the country then seemed more whole, less violated. If you know the country, you can crisscross it now, admire its bulk of wild land, look down upon it without seeing the flaw, usually, but the blemish is there: the road, the pipe—like an ugly crack on a clean windshield. But the glass is not replaceable.

I'M STATIONED AT BETTLES on the Koyukuk River, my one-man district encompassing the bulk of the Brooks Range. On this September day I have been patrolling the many lakes in the upper reaches of the Chandalar watershed, checking for bear, moose, and caribou hunters. In addition, since we handle police matters in our districts, it's my business to know who is new to the country.

I dip a wing in answer to the wave of the man on the gravel bar. By all appearances he is at home with his surroundings, with not a care in the world. It is easy to imagine the rest of the picture as I level out and head west. He likely has his winter meat, a moose, hung up in several sections, curing, some of it stripped for jerky. He will have most of his winter wood up, stacked in cords next to the cabin. The cabin, which is one of the four or five dilapidated log dwellings at the old gold-mining settlement of Caro, has no doubt been chinked with fresh moss and otherwise readied for the coming winter, which arrives early in this arctic country. The land here—soon to be frozen in a white shroud, where twenty below is considered comfortable—can be unforgiving to the inexperienced. I plan to check on this man's welfare in a month or so.

Some say you can't tell the difference once it gets twenty below zero or colder—thirty, forty, fifty, it's all the same. Well, that isn't true; those who have experienced it, been out in it, will agree. Certain things happen almost indiscernibly as the temperature drops. At thirty below, the cold seeps through heavy, normally warm clothing, and the air has a crack to it; feet will begin to freeze inside winter shoepacs in thirty minutes or so. At forty below, propane freezes, and you need to wear mittens inside a heated Super Cub; the snow underfoot is more brittle, like fine bits of frozen glass. At fifty below, there is an ache to the still air, something that pushes its way to the bone. At sixty below, it is all of the above, exaggerated; a contrail of auto exhaust hangs along a deserted highway for hours; nails in wooden houses pop in the night;

the woods are quiet, as sensible critters lay low. And at seventy below, the sap in trees snaps like rifle shots in the still woods, and splitting lake-ice booms like cannon explosions, whining as the crack reverberates at sonic speed; otherwise it is respectfully silent everywhere.

I can't explain the difference at eighty below because I've never ventured outside then, but I know that the air hangs heavy and will assault you when you simply open the door. There is a tendency to pace and to worry whether the house will continue to function against something akin to an infectious plague that lurks around and beyond the fragile windows, something that is so authoritative it has become like a living thing.

SOMETIME JUST BEFORE THANKSGIVING I make it back over to the Middle Fork. This time I am flying the smaller Piper Super Cub on skis. It is a bright day, the temperature standing around thirty below zero on the ground, not bad for this late in the year. Forty or fifty below will be the norm on a clear day in a few weeks, and in January it will occasionally dip to seventy or eighty below, ambient temperature. On my swing over the frozen river to check the cabin smoke for wind direction, I can plainly see snowshoed in the deep snow, H E L P in large letters, and a larger area packed by snowshoes as a designated landing strip. The man has heard my engine from afar and has hurried out to the river, where I can see him waving frantically. I land and taxi to where he is standing and shut the engine down. His first words when I open the door are, "You got any tobacco or cigarettes?"

It is considered rude in the Alaska bush not to be invited in for coffee or tea, especially in thirty below zero weather, but this man chooses to stand in the frigid air for our conversation, as if we were down by the corner drugstore in June. Finally I say, "You wouldn't have any coffee at the house by chance, would you?"

"No," he says. "Not even any tea left. Say, you got any groceries or anything?"

"Sure," I say, and move around to where I can get into the baggage compartment of the airplane. "Well, not anything fancy, but I've got some freeze-dried stuff here. You're welcome to it."

"That's great," he says, as he takes the packages I offer.

"You must be out of grub. Did you have a problem?"

He says he didn't accurately figure how much food they would need. They are alone, he says, just him and his new wife and their two dogs. They had been dropped off by an air taxi service out of Fort Yukon back in July, and they are not due to be picked up until sometime in April.

Already out of food in November? It sounds incomprehensible to me.

After I throw the cowl cover over the engine, he agrees to let me help him carry the few packages of rations to the cabin. I am determined to take a closer look at this setup. In the cabin, a large young woman is seated on a block of wood, facing up against and almost eclipsing a small wood-burning Yukon, or sheepherder, stove, the sort you use in a tent, not for heating a big cabin. Hunched there, she methodically chucks small kindling hacked from boards into the fire and does not particularly take notice of me as I introduce myself. Her face is dirty, her stringy hair matted, and there is a glaze in her stare.

The woman is bundled heavily against the cold, which I had not expected to find inside the cabin. A sheet of rime ice has climbed partway up the interior walls. Open spaces between the logs are two inches wide in several places, but the worst cause of draftiness is a large window opening which has been covered loosely with a piece of torn plastic through which their two huskies have free access from the outside. On the wooden table are stacked pots and pans and dishes which have not seen soap and water for some time, if ever.

One look at all this confirms my suspicions. These people are bushy. If you've ever been a little bushy, you can recognize the signs quickly. The people are lethargic, despondent, and helpless, with no basic comforts or routines established. You see it in their appearance, in their surroundings, and in their eyes. They need help, and sometimes they don't even know how badly they need it. I ask the young woman if she is cold. She says she hasn't been warm since early August. It's not humorous at the time, but I think of Robert Service's Sam McGee, who hadn't been warm since he "left Plumbtree, down in Tennessee."

They say they are down to eating nothing but dried peas. This, in a bountiful land. Although licensed and in possession of several weapons and some fishing gear, they haven't taken a moose or caribou nor caught any fish in this wild country full of fish and game.

He says they sold their in-town possessions and invested in a stake of grub, traps, guns, how-to books, and equipment. "I always wanted to live off the land while making a living trapping fur," he says.

But he hasn't set a trap, nor ventured more than a hundred yards from the cabin, according to what sign I see.

Rather than cut down and split up the large dead spruce trees surrounding them, they have torn out the flooring of the old cabins for firewood. Their only exercise is the constant chucking of sticks into the little tent-stove when, within easy carrying distance, there are at least three good barrel stoves in the other abandoned cabins.

I ask if they are ready to leave.

"Yes."

Their return charter to Fort Yukon is paid, he says, but he doesn't have money to get back to Fairbanks, where his in-laws live. He figures he will sell his guns and traps in Fort Yukon to get airfare. He offers his new .44 Magnum revolver to me for a third its value and says he'll probably have to leave his traps due to limited space on the plane. I refuse his revolver, but give him a fair price for the hundred or so traps and tell him to keep his guns until he gets to Fairbanks, where he can get a decent price for them. I leave the rest of my freeze-dried food and tell them I'll call Fort Yukon Air Service for their charter as soon as I get back to Bettles. Within three days they are out of there.

I swing back by in a week or so to pick up the traps. In a knapsack by the door are three frozen, feathered, undrawn grouse, which had been killed sometime over the past few months.

I resent the hunter. I resent
that I have led him here, to this,
a holy place in my mind.

CHAPTER SIXTEEN

A Guiding Experience

I sit on a hillside. It is September, well into my third season of guiding hunters for a living. The early frosts strike at night; the new thin snow—white dust terminating the summer hills—is bright on higher peaks; the blueberries are ripe; the fall sienna shades, yellow, red, orange, and brown, are prominent throughout the mountain brush along the sloped tundra. Bugs are gone—the black gnats, whitesocks, no-see-ums, mosquitoes. Lungs breathe clean sky, an invisible air.

In my thoughts I wonder what I'm doing here. Not what I'm doing out in the open hills, but what I'm doing guiding hunters for a few bucks a day, hunters who may not cherish where they are, nor value the animals they take. Is my guiding them a prostitution? Having lost my own compulsion to hunt for sport, I nevertheless continue for a price. I'm uncertain of the quality of my own convictions.

I think of what I've seen over the years, closely associated with hunters of all sorts. On this hill, I imagine I'm just tired of the aura of the hunt. I know there must be something beyond hunting, something on a higher plane. But I have never been in sync with anti-hunters. I haven't respected their opinions because the majority have never hunted. They don't understand the need, or the craving for the chase. Now I wonder if I am in sync with anyone. Maybe some of the anti-hunters have in fact hunted; maybe they are already on a higher plane, like Henry Thoreau, who in his youthful wisdom wrote: "He goes thither at first as a hunter and fisher, until at last, if he has the seeds of a better life in him, he distinguishes his better objects, as a poet or naturalist it may be, and leaves the gun and fish-pole behind."

MY GERMAN HUNTER AND I have climbed high into the Alaska Range peaks—the heads of canyons, creeks and draws—high where they pinch together on slopes almost not grassy because of the steepness and the new rock. Up where any small draw within a stone's throw will lead you into rivers each of great size and far apart from one another. The German is a wealthy man of my age from West Germany and speaks some English. I speak German out of a dictionary. We get along, mostly. I sense a common bond because of our age and, strangely, because of the bitter war between our fathers and our countries. We, the children of that war, impressed and indoctrinated to fear the enemy, are now old enough to attempt to forget the prejudices of our brain-washed societies.

He tells me about his experience with the occupying enemy; how, while lying in bed with the mumps, he hears the soldiers entering his house. His mother and neighbors have been fearful that the Russians will arrive before the Americans (his father is a Nazi prisoner in a Siberian gulag). Downstairs, the soldiers rummage through the house and shout in a

strange language, and he lies there waiting as boots tramp up
the stairs to his room in the loft. The door opens. A black
American soldier enters. Their eyes meet. The soldier smiles,
then takes an orange from his pack and gives it to him. My
hunter says he knew then that it would be all right. There are
tears in his eyes when he says this, but perhaps only because
of the cold wind along the slope.

The German wants a nice Dall sheep and we have seen
several, though none within our reach. They are alert animals;
eyesight is their greatest protection. They are at ease in their
environment, but vigilant, and won't be where you think they
should be after a lengthy stalk, unless careful thought is given
to the project from start to finish. I glass the far ridges and
slopes carefully, picking apart the terrain in sections, concentrating on the nooks and crannies. Although stark white
against the green, brown, or gray of the hills, wild sheep may
often appear out of nowhere, in places you've been searching
carefully. They may be bedded down in a slight swale, not
discernible even with the binoculars unless you catch the flick
of an ear. I rest my eyes and take in the atmosphere and
grandeur of the Range. From here you can see Denali to the
northeast and several ten-thousand-foot peaks below it which
look like foothills in comparison. The air is sharp, clean.

I think about having quit my job as a wildlife officer more
than two years before. The business of guiding hunters and
fishermen, and hiring on with a security company to patrol
the trans-Alaska pipeline during the winter months, seemed
like a good chance to branch out and have an independent
occupation of my own. After sixteen years in law enforcement, I had become disillusioned with the politics permeating
the upper levels of state government. But although I didn't

realize it clearly at the time, the real reason I left was probably that same old affliction that prompted me to leave New Mexico in 1969: a claustrophobic association with office areas. I needed to break out of the cage once again.

Maybe quitting had been a mistake, maybe not. One thing certain, I was learning something about commercial hunting and sportfishing from the inside looking out, and I was seeing firsthand how the oil industry was beginning to affect the Alaska wilderness. More significantly, though, I was learning something about myself.

PERHAPS THERE ARE no sheep on that far slope after all. I use the spotting scope—there are white specks along the ridgeline. It'll be a tough hike, just to get close enough to see if a legal ram is there. We work our way around after several hours of climbing and angling. We come in from above a healthy full-curl ram, where he rests ruminating, watching the slopes below for signs of danger. If he were contemplating, he would be thinking that it is a lovely day and that the valley below is pacific; no danger is apparent. But he probably does not contemplate; he only knows there is no danger at the present moment—down the slope, below in the valley.

We take the ram. Head and horns with cape, boned out meat, stuffed tightly into large moose pack; heavy load. Will the hunter take my rifle and some of the gear: tripod with spotting scope, rain slickers? No, he is already far down the mountain, thinking of something else. It will be two loads for me. Six miles each way. It is already late, so I'll come back for the second load tomorrow. He will stay in camp and bathe and maybe read. It's a service he has paid for. Why should I expect him to be a hunting companion?

A few bucks a day. What if it were megabucks a day? It would be no different. I resent the hunter. I resent that I have led him here, to this, a holy place in my mind. Maybe he does appreciate where he is; maybe he cherishes it in another language. Could I be wrong, and could he be thinking I am the one not valuing this pristine wilderness? I resent him anyway. I think I should have one of my children up here on this hunt; up here close to God in these peaks. I do not regret killing the ram then, only that this stranger has done it and not someone I care about, or no one at all. Yes, my guiding is prostitution.

A bear has been in our camp; a black bear by the look of the tracks. He has torn a hole in the canvas roof of the tent-cabin and strewn things about; bitten several cans searching for something sweet, scattering flour and feathers. My hunter has a license tag for a black bear. Maybe this bruin will come back. He does. A fat, black bear looks in the window at us; we look at him and run out into the blue night in our underwear, rifles at the ready. The bear runs into the trees before the hunter can adjust his shooting staff for placing the correct shot. I'm thinking that this kill right in the yard will make up for the twelve-mile pack trip for the sheep. But I'm also thinking there is an absurdness to it all.

The hunter stays in camp the next day waiting for the bear to return. I know that is unlikely to happen during the open day, and I make my final pack for the rest of the gear. That evening we climb a ridge where we can look down into the camp and surrounding area. We sit and meditate on the surroundings.

THAT FIRST WINTER away from my job as a wildlife officer, I was in the arctic Brooks Range, a familiar place for me. I had been there on wildlife patrol assignments and had pronounced memories of flying the peaks like an errant bird and camping on isolated gravel bars along clear rivers with forgotten names. But this new job gave a different perspective. This was a pipeline construction camp, one of many; a camp of some fourteen hundred workers, situated on the north fork of the Koyukuk River.

A great bustle was going on: bulldozers, ditchdigging machines, brilliant lights through the gray haze of fifty-below-zero ice fog, hundreds of eighteen-wheel tractor-trailers night and day boiling haul-road dust out across the frozen trees and snow, helicopters, C-130 cargo planes—a din reverberating throughout the valley. All within the shadow of Sakukpak Mountain, a three-thousand-foot giant of rock thrust up and out, imposing within an imposing land; a place of ancient spirits, with old burial grounds at its base; a place that had known only peace and quiet for hundreds of thousands of years.

There I was, walking the halls of a metallic camp on night patrol checking for furnace leaks, breaking up fights and gambling games, and rattling doorknobs. Twelve hours a night, seven nights a week, for nine weeks at a time.

Now and then though, after midnight along the frozen river just beyond camp, I would find a peace, in spite of the constant hum of diesel generators. There I could listen to the creaks and groans of river ice and the gurgles below; there the trees loomed black against the white of snow and a bluish night, and in the powdered crust along the river I could perhaps see the track of a solitary wolf. Out there, beyond the camp, the river was still wild, and with concentrated effort I could image away the sounds of the camp and believe myself in the heart of the Brooks Range I remembered from before.

THE HUNTER has become restless. He thinks we should be traipsing about the countryside, looking for the bear. I know we should wait. He begins to fuss about the wind direction. I tell him that I know what I am doing. He fusses some more. We are not getting along. He understands that I am upset with him. We sit in an angry silence.

The bear walks out into the open behind the camp, about two hundred yards from where we sit. The hunter empties his rifle at him, reloads and empties it again. He does not touch the bear, who by then is across the far threads of a glacial river and heading for another mountain. It suits me fine. Guiding is not for me. I have made decisions about that earlier in the day. It is a reclamation of my wicked soul.

Bob was a killer of animals.
Above everything else on God's
own earth, he loved to kill.

CHAPTER SEVENTEEN

Bandit Bob:

An Aberration

It is in that same fall of the year when I returned to work for the state that Fish and Wildlife trooper Dick Dykema flies over Bandit Bob as he is pouring gasoline on his own airplane.

Dick circles and watches Bob trail the aviation gas out away from the Super Cub. Bob keeps turning his head away from the circling airplane, hiding his face. But after chasing Bandit Bob for years, Dick figures he would know old Bob even in the dark. When he still refuses to look up, Dick drops down low, cuts the throttle, opens a side window, and hollers, "Hi, Bob, how you doin'?"

Startled, Bob looks up, then giving a little wave, steps over and lights a match to the fuel he has trailed away from the plane. The whole thing goes up in a ball of flame. Bob stands there, now defiantly shaking his fist at Dick, while Dick circles, transfixed, disbelieving. Bob's client, a German hunter, stands off to one side, no doubt convinced that he has made a poor choice this year in a hunting guide, and no doubt afraid of what this crazy American is going to do next. The German says later that Bob had a fit when he saw the game warden's plane; that Bob rolled on the ground, and that he "ate the dirt in big bites."

The hunter need not have been afraid. It was just Bob's style. Get caught in the act of illegally killing a bull moose by use of an airplane? Just burn the airplane to keep the state from getting it. We had already taken two or three of his airplanes over the past few years, and there would be another one or two later. Where Bob came up with the money for more airplanes I have no idea. I'm not sure I want to know. And as far as eating the dirt, well, what can I say? While awaiting his hour in court, Bob scribbled something on a piece of paper and left it on Dick's desk. It said, "In every silver lining there's a black cloud."

As long as Bandit Bob is alive, he'll probably be out there somewhere killing something—or stealing something. A few years before the dirt-eating episode, when I was stationed at McGrath, I awoke one morning to discover that the extension cord and emergency locator beacon were missing from my state airplane. Three other cords and another beacon were missing from around town. A snowstorm during the night had wiped out any tracks from around the airplanes. I figured the thief was one of the local kids—even had a good idea who. I had not realized that Bandit Bob had been in town that night, nor was I aware then he had failed to pay the bill for himself and two of his hunters at the local lodging establishment. I don't remember if it was hunting season or not, but it makes no difference. Bob hunted all year.

Not long after that, a fellow officer called from the

Anchorage office: they had found my locator beacon in Bandit Bob's airplane. It seems Bob had killed a grizzly bear out of season, and when he went back to retrieve the hide, a wildlife officer popped out of the brush and nabbed him, seizing his plane. I forget which of his planes that was, but anyway, there was my beacon, the state inventory number scratched on the bottom.

Then a big lodge out on the Susitna River, closed up for the winter, was burglarized of all its trophy animal heads and hides, scores of them. Where were they recovered? In Bandit Bob's attic.

The interesting thing was, Bob was such a likable person. You couldn't help but like him. He was a nice guy—still is, I suppose—but he was a thief, among other flaws. I don't know if Bob was lucky or unlucky. He was caught so many times that you might say he was unlucky. But managing to stay out of jail for the rest of his life was pure luck. I think the judges felt sorry for him, he had such a hangdog look.

His bad-luck/good-luck life was in full swing the day he decided to fly from Kodiak Island across the open sea to the mainland of the Kenai Peninsula in a single-engine airplane. It was also a day of bad weather. I believe his daughter was with him. Bob just climbed up on top of the rotten weather, above the clouds, and kept going. The engine quit on him somewhere out over the water and above the clouds. That was the bad luck. You've heard of a snowball's chance in hell—well, that's what chance Bob had of getting out of that situation alive. The monotonous drone of an engine—in comforting cadence with your heartbeat when you're out over water or above the clouds—can awaken you to stark fear when it sputters to dead silence and the prop slowly windmills, or freezes as an inanimate object immediately in front of the windscreen. But as Bob glided somewhat like a brick down out of the clouds, he found a fishing boat right there, the only one for many miles. Bob just put the plane in the drink and was promptly fished out.

Bob was a killer of animals. Above everything else on God's own earth, he loved to kill. This is not a common thing. The majority of hunters don't go out in the woods with that single purpose of mind (even though their spouses might not agree). It is not a mania with them to kill. I've known of only a few people like that, and Bandit Bob was the worst. For these few like Bob, it didn't matter if they had a hunting partner; they didn't care about companionship, nor the outdoor experience. Like a psychopath, the true killer kills for the killing.

I suppose this sort of person may have been looked upon with reverence in the old days. He would have been constantly hunting and killing and bringing in meat for the entire village. But he would be an aberration today. Bandit Bob is an aberration. We finally grew tired of catching him; there comes a point at which you have to spread some of the budget around to others.

I'VE BEEN A HUNTER most all my days, but I'm still not sure what makes a hunter tick. There's a motivation there, that's certain. And a predictableness. Hunters are predictable somewhat like automobile drivers are predictable. Drivers get behind the wheel—it doesn't matter what their status or profession is in real life—they get in the driver's seat and assume another persona, often becoming clones of what they believe a driver ought to be.

That's the way it is with hunters. You meet them in the field and you have no way of knowing who they are; they've reverted to being hunters—good, bad, or otherwise. Now, don't take this as any sign of bitterness with me—I'm only stating it as a fact—but I've never seen any activities in which ordinarily honest people are more tempted to lie, cheat, and steal than hunting and fishing. But like an old-time warden once told me, "Remember, they ain't all bad, so treat 'em with a little respect. It might be the only time they ever meet a game warden. But watch out, and don't forget, every hunter ain't a son of a bitch, but every son of a bitch goes huntin'."

The impulse to hunt builds up in urban hunters. It becomes a frantic thing when the limited hunting season approaches. There may be only a few days off from work—a short span in which to squeeze all the nomadic hunter's juices. No wonder hunters sometimes become a menace on the highways, in the woods, and to each other.

But a hunter who has the chance to go out often into the woods usually becomes more relaxed with the surroundings. The hunter may even find that the fresh air and open space is all that is sought, and may become engrossed in examining those favorite haunts more closely—feeling a reverence, in fact. Could it be that the hunt is just a means to experience a place which only the soul still understands?

It's no small thing to be raised a hunter. Hunting may well have been a family custom, and for some people, it can be a burden to carry. You are expected to be successful in the hunt; if not, the hunt is deemed a failure. And what does that make you? But if you do well, you're rewarded with acceptance into the fraternity and the feeling of elation at succeeding at a pursuit considered by many to be natural, acceptable, and expected. And if you happen to be a member of an aboriginal tribe deep within the Amazon watershed, there's no doubt that it is natural and acceptable. But if you are a member of a modern urban society, it may no longer be—and you may decide you need to think about it.

But as for Bandit Bob: God may want to have a personal chat with Bob.

*On this hunt—the hunt that
nails them—we have our blood
brother in their midst.*

CHAPTER EIGHTEEN

A Far North Sting

The guide and his client crouch in a patch of snow as the big
grizzly surges up the hill toward them, trashing the willows,
scattering the snow, and blowing snot. The gap is narrowed
to less than a hundred yards.

"Don't shoot till I tell you to," the guide says, "and when
you shoot, place your shot into the shoulder. We need to
break him down."

The hunter settles the crosshairs of his scope unwaver-
ingly centered on the loping bear, his heart pounding in
his throat.

But this is not a charging bear; this bear has not even seen
the men. He is a bear running for his life from an airplane
persistently boring in from behind, blasting him with its
whining prop and backfiring Lycoming engine all the way up
the hill from the frozen creek bottom, where he was rudely
flushed from his bed.

"Shoot him now," the guide says, as the panting, slobbering bruin angles toward the two men, now within sixty yards.
The hunter complies, dropping the bear with one shot. In a
snarling, fit-throwing rage, the grizzly bites at the pain as

though it were a stinging insect. But he is unable to scare it away, and he finally succumbs to the overwhelming power of it all, breathing his last in the fading snow patches of late spring.

"Put another one in him for good measure," the guide says, while the chase plane flies off to land on a faraway ridge. Then the guide, well practiced, begins to quickly skin the bear. The client casually snaps pictures of the bear and the guide, also taking overlapping panoramic photos of the surrounding horizon. Then he surreptitiously hangs a small, dull object behind a willow branch nearby. It is a homing device. I will take it off the branch myself in a few days.

The client is Nando Mauldin, an undercover U.S. Fish and Wildlife Service agent, at that time based in Washington, D.C. The shooting of this bear is the event that will break the back of an illegal guiding operation that had plagued western Alaska for years.

SUPPLY AND DEMAND. And greed. Over the years, several Alaska hunting guides have succumbed to the pressure imposed by the occasional unhappy hunter who has failed to bag the animal he has come for. The guide feels the need to produce—and if the price is right, some will produce. Taking game with the help of an airplane becomes the easy way out, and what better way to select the best animal in thousands of square miles of country in only one day? Why spend days and days scouring a few square miles of country on foot with only one or two hunters, and no guarantee of a kill? A one-day airplane hunt can produce the best of all the bears that are spotted, and the hunter can enjoy the comforts of a lodge at the end of the day. In this manner a heap of bears can be taken during a season that is only open for fifteen days.

We game wardens had been stymied for years in trying to stop this activity. Up until 1972 an indifferent Fish and Game Department hierarchy, for whom our enforcement division worked at that time, would not listen to our pleas for more productive enforcement techniques. In 1970, we asked for support to use some undercover hunters. The reply of the Fish and Game commissioner to a small group of us at a meeting in Fairbanks was, "We're not playing that cloak-and-dagger shit."

So the bandit guides—I prefer to separate them from the legitimate guides by that designation—continued to have their field day with Alaska's big game. It was big bucks for them. Simple arithmetic: more bears, more bucks.

We were ineffective in those days, a joke to many of the big-time operators. We continued to bring most of our cases and arrests against the general hunting public, while the bandit guides seemed to be untouchable. Catching one in the act was next to impossible.

Then a fortunate thing happens. In 1972, April to be exact, the governor, "Uncle" Bill Egan, becomes angered with our enforcement division over pay differences. He considers the division a "loose cannon" and through the power of his office simply gives us the choice of moving over to the State Troopers or of being fired, the lot of us. It is the biggest favor he can do for us, and for wildlife protection (although he was not thinking of the wildlife when he did it). We are finally where we belong: in an organization where the priority is professional law enforcement and the politics are minimal.

Within two years, after the initial transition miseries that accompany moving a whole division in with another, we have the support and money we need for undercover operations.

Meanwhile, I've been asked to move into Anchorage, a big city by Alaska standards. Once again I'm giving up the outdoors for the desk, fighting rush-hour traffic to and from work, facing four walls that can close in if I let them. But I don't. I break away into the field as much as possible to keep the cobwebs out of my gut. From detachment supervisor I am pushed up to commander of sport fish and game enforcement statewide after a year and a half.

In this new position I am given the authority to initiate a covert agreement with the U.S. Fish and Wildlife Service, working through its special agent in charge of Alaska, Ray Tremblay. The Service already has a few well-trained, experienced officers established as undercover agents in various parts of the country. My old friend Nando Mauldin—one of my training officers when I was a rookie in New Mexico, and a fellow connoisseur of venison stew—is now one of these agents. After twenty years with New Mexico, he has gone to work for the feds.

The work in setting up some hunts begins. No smart outlaw guide is going to book a hunter he is suspicious of, and the really prolific ones already have plenty of bookings. Why take on an unknown, unreferenced client? Most of the guides run background checks on prospective clients—and some of them later wished they had done a better job of it.

Jim Nutgrass, eventually in charge of the state Fish and Wildlife Investigations Section, takes over the state's end of the preparations, and through more than a year of hard work with the federal undercover section, he connects on some initial bookings. Hence, Nando Mauldin the client.

NANDO'S GUIDE and the guide's partner have been taking twelve to fifteen bears in a fifteen-day hunting season and have been doing it year after year. There is no legitimate way they can take that many bears and stay within the law. They have to be taking them by direct use of aircraft. Laws have been enacted to prevent this "unfair chase" by making it unlawful to take a bear on the same day a hunter has been airborne. In addition, it is in violation of state and federal laws to harass wildlife with an aircraft.

We have been staking out guides suspected of this sort of activity for years, watching their camps and lodges, recording the comings and goings, trying to match hunters leaving in the morning with those returning with freshly killed bears in the evening. We are seldom successful. The guides simply set up a temporary camp after taking a bear, overnight the hunter and assistant guide, and pick them up the next day.

A law is enacted requiring the registration of a specified number of camps that a guide can maintain. Bear hides cannot be transported except from these designated camps to designated airports, and guided hunters cannot hunt from other than registered camps. The bandit guides work around this: they fly the hunters into the registered camps after making the kill. The only chance they take is being seen letting the hunter and assistant out of the airplane near where a bear is spotted, then driving the bear to them.

We can't stake out every hunting camp in the country. Nor can we monitor the thousands of square miles of bear country. But we can locate the best areas of bear concentration and send in a camouflaged staked-out officer to watch. On occasion this works, but it has not worked in capturing Nando's guides. However, on this hunt—the hunt that nails them—we have our blood brother in their midst.

Nando is prepared for at least a few days of some semblance of hunting. Even he would not have believed the sequence of events if he had not been there to watch them unfold.

He is picked up by the guide in Anchorage and flown several hundred miles out to the lodge. They overnight there, awaiting the arrival of the other guide and two more hunters. Over dinner and drinks that night, Nando volunteers to delay his hunt so that the other hunters, two doctors from Los Angeles, can hunt first. This allows Nando to remain in a position to document enough evidence about the doctors' hunts to later use in bringing a case against the guides, if the hunts are successful.

Then it's Nando's turn. He and the two guides take off in two Piper Super Cubs and fly a beeline for a hundred and thirty miles to the west, completely out of the game management unit the guides normally hunt. It is difficult for Nando to keep track of where they are in hundreds of square miles of wilderness, none of which he has ever been in. He cannot afford to appear too interested in their whereabouts, but he knows he will need to remember where they have been. He keeps notes on the inside of a matchbook cover. They eventually land on a hilltop, where a tent has previously been set up that shelters two sets of airplane skis, a small amount of camping gear, and extra aviation fuel. The planes are taxied to the edge of the snow, where the guides remove the tundra-tired wheels from both airplanes and replace them with skis. They refuel and take off.

"We located several bear," Nando says later, "and circled them to determine the size and condition of the pelts. One was a large blond boar who reared up on his back legs and ran, reaching for our airplane as we flew just overhead. The guide said he wasn't big enough."

In a short while they locate the hapless chocolate-colored grizzly in the creek bottom. The guide says to Nando, "That is your bear." The scene is set for a quick kill, the two bandits discussing the plan of attack over their radios.

"When we landed," Nando says, "we used every foot of the little patch of snow, sliding right up to within a few feet of the end of it."

Nando is careful to not make suggestions at any point regarding the hunt; to simply allow the guide to instruct him on taking the bear in the manner of their normal procedures. "I felt somewhat dirty," he says later, "for having to kill such a fine animal to get at individuals profiting at the expense of the resource."

After skinning the bear, the guide takes off with it, meeting the other airplane several miles away to exchange the cargo. Nando is left with only his rifle and camera. At that point he has a twinge of concern that if he is suspected to be an undercover officer, he might well be left where he stands. He puts the thought out of his mind and busies himself taking more photos. When the guide returns, a reverse of the morning's flight takes place: back to the tent, change the skis to wheels, and back to the lodge.

A nice, cozy wilderness bear hunt. A nice, cozy profit. Three trophy bears in three days. Make ready for more hunters! But the profit is destined to be somewhat restricted for these two guides.

THERE ARE REPORTS to complete, complaints to file, arrest warrants and seizure warrants to serve, interviews to conduct. Emotions run high. One of the two guides threatens to run over the officers and agents with the airplane they come to seize. He sits in the cockpit, threatening to start the engine while one of the officers stands under the prop, hopefully to prevent takeoff.

It is several days before investigator Jack Jordan and I can head out to investigate the crime scene, a necessary step in corroborating Nando's statements. We have a tracking device on the Super Cub; a fairly good idea of the general area of the kill, thanks to Nando's observations; and a panoramic photo of the country.

There is only one problem (but it has been anticipated): what snow there was is almost gone and I will have to find an area to land on wheels, preferably close by. It takes a while to locate the kill. There is a ridge above it that looks landable, but I use up valuable fuel in looking it over. My concern is not so much in landing safely, but in being able to take off once on the ground. The wind is ideal for landing, coming straight down the steep ridge. But because it is steep, the takeoff will have to be downhill, unfortunately also downwind. Under certain light wind conditions, this can work out, but conditions are not that way. I know that the afternoon or late evening winds generally switch to moving up the canyons. It is with this hope in mind that I finally commit us to landing.

We take duplicate photos of Nando's panorama and the bear carcass, gather an empty shell casing, locate a bullet by aid of a metal detector—it entered the bear and traveled several yards up the inside of an intestine before coming to rest—and retrieve the homing device from the bush where Nando left it. We have plenty of time; the wind has not switched. By late afternoon, however, the wind dies down, and we make it off the ridge in one full-throttled galloping piece.

THE TWO GUIDES have a lot at stake. So do we. If this case does not finish them, we are out of ideas. They hire a battery of attorneys to sift and chew their way through the state and federal charges and evidence. But it is a tight case.

Meanwhile, the feds gain information that death threats are being made, that a contract is out for Nando. A source is traced back to Detroit, to an organized crime family hit man. Nando is ordered to leave the D.C. area and assume a new identity until the long court battle is over. At one of the hearings in Alaska, a defense attorney seeks to gain favor with the judge by pointing out that Nando is apparently armed while testifying and that there are "sixteen armed guards in the courtroom, your honor, and how is my client supposed to get a fair hearing!"

"There have been so many death threats over this case that even I am armed," the judge says. "I don't think the fact that the witness is armed will affect his ability to tell the truth. . . . I suggest if you have further questions for this witness, you proceed with them."

The two guides are convicted. They serve jail time, lose two airplanes, are assessed a sizable fine, and lose their guide licenses and exclusive guide areas. We are in business! The rest of the bandit guides are now running scared. Many of the borderline bandits switch back to legitimate operations. Not many of them can afford taking chances.

He still smells the hot stink of the breath and feels the grip of the bear's teeth scraping his skull.

CHAPTER NINETEEN

Among the Bears

The constant threat of bears could change your attitude about things, I suppose. Although I lived alone for three wilderness months in a small tent at Nuka Bay as a young man, it was not in the company of bears—only muttering porcupines, who up close in the black of night sound like bears to a green ear. But for wildlife officers on stakeout assignment, bears come with the territory. It takes a certain type of person to put up with the conditions of stakeout duty in order to catch bandit bear guides.

It was my job to put these stakeouts out, to take care of their needs if weather permitted, and to pick them up at the end of their assignment, which often lasted for up to two weeks. One officer, an ordinarily tough outdoorsman, had literally become sick to his stomach from fear when a squad of giant Alaska Peninsula brown bears bemoaned his presence in their Clark River domain by stepping on the tent ropes, growling, fighting with each other, and sitting on his tent during a miserable night. The officer said if I hadn't come in and taken him out of there when I did, he would have started an almost impossible trek out himself.

The Bush

I had learned to respect the brown bears—the grizzlies—early in my Alaska career.

My NEW WORK IN ALASKA first brought me to a district south of Nenana in the Interior. I had not been there a month when I rented three horses, packed up two of them, threw my saddle on the third, and set out to spend ten days patrolling the Dall sheep hunting season in the Wood River country northeast of Mt. McKinley National Park.

Late the second day out, after struggling through two feet of fresh snow while working my way over a high pass, I break out of the timber onto the first open gravel bar of the braided Wood River. It must be ten o'clock at night, although it's still not dark, and I've put in a hard ride of about fourteen hours. It is misting rain here in the valley, and I begin looking for a place along the edge of the timber to camp. A rest, with grain for the horses and a big spruce log fire for me, will be good for our spirits.

A young Toklat grizzly emerges from the trees about seventy yards off to our left and ahead of us. He hasn't seen us yet, but the horses have spotted him, and there are three sets of ears pointing very attentively in his direction. I am not particularly alarmed, although I can see that the grizzly's angle of travel will soon intersect ours.

It doesn't take me long to realize there is a distinct personality difference between the black bear and the grizzly (also known as the brown bear in the coastal areas of the state). I'd heard that the brown/grizzly was a more aggressive animal, but passed it off as only an opinion of some. I'd met bears on the trail before—black bears, while on horseback in New Mexico. They always beat a quick retreat. I have no reason to believe this Wood River grizzly will react any differently. I enter the scene confidently. The bear is also confident when he finally spots us. He alters his line of travel, heads more directly toward us, and quickens his pace across the sand and gravel and little rivulets of water.

The only ones not confident up until then are the horses, who have been raised in grizzly country and exhibit a certain well-founded apprehension. The two pack horses begin to bunch up with the horse I am riding, their heads almost in the saddle with me. I hold the lead rope to one, while the second pack horse is tied by his lead rope to the pack saddle of the first. Bunching up in that manner I am concerned about the slack ropes dangling about their legs. With the second pack horse in my left lap and the first pack horse in my right lap, the lead rope between them is working its way up under the tail of my saddle horse—a situation destined to cause a wreck of the worst sort.

The grizzly by now has quickened his pace to a hopping trot, bounding in our direction as if he has been waiting all day for us to get there, like an old family dog happy to see the kids coming home from school. When he is within twenty yards of me, he begins popping his teeth and hissing; within fifteen yards, he starts to crow-hop sideways toward us. He reminds me then of a mean dog, the sort you find along your newspaper route. Except bigger.

I sense that the horses are on the verge of hightailing it out of there, leaving me sitting alone on the gravel bar with an ill-tempered grizzly. I decide right then that the wildest bronc in the world couldn't separate me from my saddle.

We reach a three-foot-deep channel in the river, and the horses quickly bolt across, me along for the ride. The grizzly has come within ten yards of us but stops at the water's edge, where he continues to pop his teeth and seems to be saying, ". . . and don't come back." I am shaken by the experience, and it is several more miles and well after dark before I make camp. I do not sleep well that night.

The next day, several miles downriver, I locate our new patrol cabin back on the edge of the timber. It is a small plywood shack without windows, but it is a place out of the weather (and safe from grizzly bears, I figure). A few days later, while I'm away, a grizzly and her cub stop by the shack, which has a door that swings inward. The sow and her cub shove the door open, bite holes in all the cans to test the contents, tear open pancake mix, flour, and sugar, and generally raise hell. But the real hell is not raised until the old sow realizes the door has swung shut. Rather than thoughtfully opening it, she apparently, from the looks of things, makes about three turns around the track and takes out the biggest part of one wall, a full panel of plywood. I salvage what I can and make camp wherever night finds me after that.

I HAVE TRIED TO UNDERSTAND why some people can associate in mutual comfort with aggressive bears. It may be that these people do not exude aggressiveness themselves. Maybe they are people closer to the earth in soul and spirit than most of the rest of us.

Dr. Adolph Murie had spent something over fifty years in and around McKinley Park. A naturalist and biologist, he narrowed his research mainly to the study of wolves and bears in that area, spending much time over the years walking among the grizzlies. When I met him, not long after my brush with the Wood River bear that first fall in Alaska, he said he had never met with any serious aggression from a bear—although he knew of authentic accounts involving other people—and that he never carried a gun in the field.

I met Dr. Murie by surprise one day while driving on patrol toward Wonder Lake. I had my young son with me and had pulled up to a cabin along the Toklat River. A white-haired gentleman came out and introduced himself as "Murie."

"Not *the* Murie," I said.

He replied, "You must mean my brother, Olaus."

I had not meant Olaus, although I knew his brother was also a prominent naturalist. This humble man, Adolph, invited us in for coffee, and we met his wife, Louise, and the well-known wildlife photographer Charles Ott, who also had many years working among the grizzlies of McKinley Park. In the course of our conversation it was interesting to hear from both Murie and Ott that neither had any fear of contact with bears and that they had experienced but few encounters that caused them undue concern.

I asked if they knew why they seemed to be accepted by bears, when other people, including other experienced outdoorsmen, had been chased and mauled or killed. Neither could voice any reason for this phenomenon.

It seems likely to me that bears sense an aggressive nature in some people and that they react not only to what they perceive as a person's fear of them, but to their own fear of certain people who they sense are a threat. They apparently never feared Murie or Ott, or at least never felt threatened by them. It is true that the McKinley bears are not subject to the hunting and harassment experienced by bears in other areas, but the park still has had its share of maulings over the years, including that of a park ranger.

There were a few attacks in New Mexico by black bears, but most notorious bear attacks occur in Alaska and Canada, and they usually involve the brown/grizzly. Hardly a year goes by in Alaska that there aren't some maulings by this bellicose bruin. It's this aggressiveness that gives the bear its popularity with the hunter: man against ferocious beast, with photos depicting the proud hunter with his trophy Alaskan brown bear. Some of the stories told along with the photos stretch the imagination. There are scores of documented cases of bear attacks on humans—but if all the stories accompanying trophy bear kills were accurate, there would be many thousands of such attacks. Yes, the bear is an aggressor, but in most cases the hunter has precipitated the attack, if there is one. However, it does not pay to come between a bear and its kill, or between a sow and her cubs, and there are times when the attacks seem unexplainable.

AL THOMPSON, who was later one of my fellow officers on the Kenai Peninsula, found out something about bears that chew on people.

Al had taken some time off from his work as a game warden one fall and went moose hunting up into the hills between the Kenai River and Tustamena Lake. He and his wife, Joyce, had all their gear on their backs. They were traveling light and covered seventeen miles up the Funny River Trail that first day out. Al planned to take a bull with his bow, and he hoped that Joyce could take one with her 30.06 rifle. If successful they would hang the quartered meat and have it packed out on horseback by a local outfitter. Al took along his .44 Magnum revolver for bear protection.

That first evening they set up camp by building a log lean-to, covering the front with Visqueen plastic to ward off the September frost. They banked their nearby campfire with logs to keep it burning most of the night. They had seen fresh bear sign in several places on the trek in, and when they turned in for the night, Al kept both the aught-six and the pistol near his side—the handgun laid out on a yellow paper towel for better visibility. This was a habit he would follow each night.

For the next two days he and Joyce enjoyed a leisurely hunt, passing up several legal bulls not up to their expectations. But mainly they soaked up the experience of the scenes and scents that the birch, aspen, and spruce forests and the blueberry-brushed hillsides provide during an Alaska fall.

It is late on their third night in camp when Al is awakened by something near the lean-to. He silently awakens Joyce, asking her to lie still, while he fumbles for the rifle. The "something" crashes through the plastic on top of them before Al has time to react. It is a large bear. The aught-six is knocked from Al's grasp. Trying to protect Joyce, he manages a choke hold on the bear with his left arm while groping for the rifle or his revolver with his right hand. There's not enough time. The bear rakes Al's back open with claws the length of a man's fingers. Al repeatedly strikes the animal in the muzzle with his free right fist, which only further enrages the thrashing bruin, who now wrenches loose and bites Al through the left forearm. He then begins to gnaw on Al's head, trying to get a grip on the scalp or crush the skull.

Through the clamor and roar, Joyce frantically searches for one of the guns, to no avail. The bear has seized Al in its jaws and a foreleg and carries him down the hill about twenty-five yards, where he drops him on the spruce needles and renews the mauling. Al knows he desperately needs to try something else. Somehow he thinks clearly enough to decide he should force himself to relax, to play dead. It works. The bear leaves.

Knowing that the bear will probably return if he moves, but worried that Joyce will be its next victim, Al gets up and fumbles through the dark to the camp. Joyce is shaken but not injured. She is startled at what she sees. Her husband and partner of more than fifteen years stands in the dim light of the fire, a ragged and bloody mess, the front of his scalp gone, his left arm hanging useless, his back like the mangled flesh at a whipping post. She musters her inner strength, knowing that coolheadedness may mean life or death for them. They find the revolver, still on the yellow towel, then build up the fire as large as they can manage and brew some tea. Joyce does her best to slow Al's bleeding and bandage his wounds. In fear and shock they wait for daylight, three hours away.

There is no way out except by foot and no one nearby to assist. They leave their gear, except for the firearms, and set off down the trail. Seventeen miles. "I worried that Al would be too weak," Joyce said later, "but it was all I could do to keep up with him." The trail is torturous and slick later in the day from the thawing frost, yet they navigate it faster than when they first traveled it on the way in, an eternity ago.

Two police officers, Wayne Selden and Ron Glaser, get a call at midmorning. Their friend Al has been mauled by a bear. They jump in their car and tear out the Funny River Road. "Al and Joyce were just sitting there along the road," Ron says later, "Al all covered with blood and holding his head." Within thirty minutes they have Al at the hospital in Soldotna, with his mangled arm, deep lacerations in his back, and a six-inch-round head wound where a patch of scalp is simply gone.

That same day, Joyce, along with Glaser, Selden, and several others, return to the camp by helicopter to search for the scalp. The men are heavily armed, not knowing what to expect from the rogue bear. They form a line to search the area by grid: one step and look, another step and look. Ron says he almost steps on the scalp; it is only fifteen or twenty feet from the campsite. They place it in a saline solution to keep it fresh and head for town. The doctors sew it back on.

That night the State Trooper director calls me at home in Eagle River and says he wants me to take the Cessna 180 down to the Kenai and team up with the sergeant there to see if we can find the bear. The next day we search the area by air with the Cessna and a chartered helicopter. We find a black bear on a moose kill not far from Al's campsite. It's the only bear for miles. We decide to take it. It is one of those split-second decisions: perhaps take the wrong bear, or perhaps pass up the right one—a bear that is apparently unafraid of people and now knows that it can intimidate through aggression. Al said his attacker was a brown/grizzly, and the bear we spot is a black. But I think, *How could Al know for sure in the dark of night?*

We take the bear—kill it and haul it back to the Kenai

airport, where a Fish and Game biologist autopsies it. It is an old sow, not very big, with poor teeth and not in the best of condition. There's a piece of Visqueen plastic in her stomach. We rationalize that this is the right bear, defending the decision to kill it against any doubters who wish to doubt. This bear would have been defending her kill.

Maybe so. But Al insists it was a big brown that carried him off down the hill in its jaws without touching him to the ground. I figure, well, it's OK for Al to have the right to think he was chewed on by whatever he wants; he carries the proof of bites and lacerations on his body and the nightmares in his mind; he still smells the hot stink of the breath and feels the grip of the bear's teeth scraping his skull.

And a couple of weeks later, in broad daylight, another man afoot is mauled a few miles from Al and Joyce's campsite. The attacker is a large brown/grizzly.

Al put in a long stay in the hospital but did not lose his sense of humor. He joked that the doctors didn't even clean the spruce needles off his scalp before slapping it back on, and hadn't even checked to be sure the part in the hair was straight!

The scar on Al's forehead became a part of his character. He never hesitated to show it to the schoolkids, along with slides of animals and good stories about the outdoors. The kids loved his stories and they loved Al. I remember the little boy who said to me, "We sure like to have Mr. Thompson come and talk his stories. I liked the one where the bear ate him best of all."

Al could appreciate that kind of honesty.

*The hunter shot into the herd of caribou
with his high-powered rifle. He killed
until his ammunition ran out.*

CHAPTER TWENTY

The Meat Hunters

From the airplane I see a scattering of dead caribou—caribou shot and left to lie, fifteen of them. It is in the western arctic semi-treeless plains. The Piper Super Cub leaves a frost contrailing behind in the twenty-five below zero air; I can see it shadowed against the bright snow. I can still sense the aroma from those days of cold flight: the smell of home-tanned chopper mitts heated by the defroster on top of the instrument panel, the odor of ignited 80/87-octane fuel and of pungent nondetergent engine oil. The air is smooth; the sun etches the definition of tracks in the snow.

Two of the caribou have been salvaged; some of the others have been dragged to a central location but not eviscerated. The gases have bloated them; the birds—the ravens and Canada jays—have worked on them. The snowmachine tracks lead to a village.

One man there is the successful hunter. He had located a herd of meat; he killed the meat with his high-powered rifle; he killed until his ammunition ran out. He dressed and loaded two caribou on his sled, leaving the rest, and returned to the village. He never went back. He got drunk celebrating his accomplishment and never went back. Maybe the caribou would be closer to the village next time, maybe not. In fact, that was near the beginning of a rapid population decline in the western arctic caribou herds. Wolves, over-hunting, starvation, disease, and mismanagement would take their toll. It would be years before there was a plentiful supply for wolves or man again.

NOT MORE THAN TWENTY MILES up the Holitna River from its junction with the Kuskokwim River at the village of Sleetmute, I spot the black form of a moose contrasting with the gray-white of the river ice. The animal is seemingly in repose. But this moose is different from the other moose I have been seeing on my all-day flying patrol this January day. It is a dead moose.

Descending to three or four hundred feet off the river, I can see that it is a young bull, apparently left untouched. As I circle to land, I spot another carcass a couple of hundred yards downstream. This one has the hindquarters removed. Airplane ski tracks are visible intermittently in a few soft drifts along the hard ice of the river surface. I land off to one side to keep from disturbing what sign there is.

Once on the ground I need to make quick work of my inspection. The temperature is about forty below zero on the river, and though dressed for the cold, I know that my feet will begin to freeze after thirty minutes or so in the winter shoepacs I am wearing. Twenty-five below is about their limit. Of course, if worst comes to worst, I can dig my trail mukluks out of the emergency gear in the back of the airplane. I cover the engine with the cowl cover to retain some of its heat, a habit this time of year even if I plan only a short stop. It would not do to have a frozen-up engine out here in the middle of nowhere.

The sign on the snow reads like a book. A ski/wheel Cessna 180 or 185 dropped off two people, then took off and herded the two moose from downriver, around the bend to the two hunters waiting in ambush in the willows. Six shots total from a 30.06 and a .270 dropped both moose. The airplane then returned, the pilot helping the other two people remove the hindquarters of one bull and load it into the plane. They did not touch the second animal.

In addition to the boot prints of all three individuals, the brass cartridge cases, and the ski tracks, I find two additional items of evidence: some Kleenex with yellow decoration along the borders and a custom-made sheath-style hunting knife, left at the butchered carcass.

The kills are several days old, indicating that the poachers will not be coming back for the rest of the meat. There are several violations here: taking moose out of season, wasting game meat, harassing and herding game with an aircraft.

There are many possible places to start looking for these characters. Anchorage has the largest number of resident aircraft in the state and is a possibility. The city lies about three hundred miles away, which might explain why the poachers hadn't returned for the rest of the meat. But it's a long way to go to poach moose in the first place, and there is plenty of game much closer to town.

Bethel, with a fair number of ski-equipped airplanes, lies about a hundred and twenty miles to the southwest. There are fewer moose around Bethel, but still plenty of them closer than the Holitna country. No, my boys are going to be from around the immediate area here somewhere—somewhere, say within fifty miles, which includes some seven or eight villages.

Most of the airplanes privately owned in the bush at that time are smaller than the Cessna 180 or 185, and most people do not own the more expensive ski/wheel combination that allows the pilot to land either on snow or on a dry, hard surface. In fact, about the only ones who own this sort of plane are air taxi operators. I know most of these operators, and I doubt that any of them would be involved in such shenanigans. But it's still the best hunch.

I fly to Red Devil to talk to the nearest air taxi operator with a ski/wheel plane that size. He says he doesn't know anything about the moose, but he allows me to search his Cessna 180. A Kleenex box with yellow trimmed paper is there; a knife sheath is there; bits of blood, meat, and moose hair are there. He is cooperative. He says his son has had exclusive use of the plane for the last two weeks. We talk to the son. He admits to the crime and implicates two others, a schoolteacher and a local contractor. All three are wage earners, and are of varied ethnic background.

I need to remind myself, now and then—whenever I get the urge to blame any particular segment of the population for wasting animals—that the western European brought firearms to this country, and with them the true beginnings of large-scale waste. As far back as 1881, naturalist John Muir, while aboard the U.S. Revenue steamer *Thomas Corwin* in the Chukchi Sea off the west coast of Alaska, wrote of his fear that the native caribou had been "well-nigh exterminated within the last few years" by repeating rifles traded by whalers to the villagers for ivory, whalebone, and furs. The native

Alaskan could kill only so many caribou with a spear. The repeating rifle gave him a new ability. The snowmachine gave us all a new ability, as did the motorboat and the airplane. They allowed some people to trample on the spirit of the hunting privilege.

People waste. People in the bush, people from the city; one caribou or fifteen, one bison or millions, one passenger pigeon or all of them. All.

FROM MY PATROL AIRCRAFT I see the four quarters of a moose hanging under a spruce scaffold near the bank of a small river, the North Fork of the Kuskokwim. A camp is there. Smoke from a smudge fire floats over the meat, keeping the flies away. A wooden river skiff is tied to the bank. The handmade skiff and the lack of trash or of modern accouterments indicates this is a poor man's camp. Poor but thrifty. And it is a permanent camp, by the looks of the well-trodden ground, the size of the fire pit, and the gray of the cache poles and fish-drying racks. It is not moose season (at least by the laws made by urban dwellers); it is too early in the fall. I land on some open turf not far from the camp.

A young Athabaskan man and two small children come to meet me. We go to the camp for coffee. His wife is there, and a baby. The camp is clean, and the early sun steams the damp riverbank. There is a view from here out across the boggy flats beyond the clearwater river. You can see the rounded tops of the Telida Hills, turning gold and orange from the early fall birch. He does not mention the moose.

We visit; I want to know what he does. He lives here with

his family. He does not wish to live at Nikolai, his village several miles downriver; there is too much violence there, he says. There is too much drinking in the village, too much laziness, he says. He has lived here at this camp for three years. He traps for fur in the winter, makes his own snowshoes out of willow and sinew, traps sheefish in the summer for his winter dog feed, teaches his oldest son the things his grandfather taught him. I have the thought that he is unified with the country and, though he cannot articulate it in my language very well, I know he feels a pride in his abilities and a sense of worth in his soul. He does not have an urban education. He does, however, make himself understood to me: his honesty speaks to me through his manner, and through his eyes.

We talk about the moose. His grandfather has taught him this is the time to kill the moose for the best meat, before the rut. He does not care about the antlers; they do not even make good soup. He says he is very fortunate to have found the moose so early before the snows. He knows that the official moose season is not yet open, and he has heard there are game wardens who enforce such rules.

I tell him before I go to not leave his moose near the riverbank for everyone who flies by to see. I tell him that someone will see it and turn him in and that it will mean the loss of the meat and a month or more in jail away from his family. I tell him that if I truly come by here in real life and see a moose, I will take him to jail. I do not smile, because it is a serious thing for me. This is the first time in my career that I will overlook what in most places is a serious game violation. He does not smile either. He understands what I am saying, the totality of it. His son smiles up at me. He is too young to know what we are saying, yet he needs assurance that his father and this lawman are not so engrossed in serious talk that they forget the pleasantries of life, and that it is a good day. He reminds me of a puppy who wants me to throw a stick to fetch. I smile back.

I fly over the camp again a week later. The moose is not in sight. I waggle my wings and go on.

I sensed a respect for the land in many
of the old-timers. There was something
they had—a knowledge, or ethic—that
I wasn't ready for.

CHAPTER TWENTY-ONE

Reverence

The doorless outhouse lay over a rise and down in a swale.
You could sit there and view a little world of hillside woods:
birch and white spruce trees, willows, low-bush cranberry and
blueberry shrubs, and the white-flowered dogwood. There
were wildflowers of Nootka rose, primrose fireweed, and
western blue flag. A varied thrush had her nest on a spruce
limb within ten feet of the door opening. You could study her
features as she studied yours, attaching her black-marbled
steady eye to your every thought, or so it seemed. Her brown
form appeared like something naturally inanimate, yet her
moist eye gave truth to the vibrancy that was there. We called
her Henrietta; she hatched and raised her young next to the
privy that summer as we built our cabin. When someone
needed to go to the outhouse, they would announce: *I'm going*
to go visit Henrietta; thus their privacy was assured.

There were others like her who gravitated to this place
for the season: the red-billed arctic terns, black-capped
Bonaparte's gulls, least sandpipers, iridescent tree swallows,
and a set of mallards. A pair of red-necked grebes nested the
first couple of years we were there, just down the lake. But

they never hatched a brood. A couple of arctic loons (sometimes called Pacific loons) would sneak in and destroy the grebe eggs one at a time. A great deal of howling and commotion from the grebes and there would be one less egg. Territorial aggression. Maybe the grebes went somewhere more hospitable the next season; they didn't come back.

But the loons fared no better. They would hatch one or two chicks each year, and the bald eagles would snatch the young birds from out on the open water before they got big enough to dive. Later a pair of common loons replaced the arctics. They raised two chicks to maturity each year, both adults spending the majority of their time diving for finger-length sticklebacks, feeding the young. Dive, feed, dive, feed—mid-July to late September. The eagles tried to catch them unaware, but the older loons were too eagle-eyed for them.

The call of the common loon is described as mournful, forlorn, lonely. The sound depicts a solitary mood, it's true: the remoteness of the boreal wilderness. But to know a loon is to know that the long-noted mournful call means all is well. Is there another who speaks with such singularity in the wild? Maybe only the gray wolf.

Loons are our most ancient living bird, dating back several million years. Solid bones, not hollow like other birds, cause the loons to sit low on the water and allow them to dive to great depths with ease. I sometimes look at them and realize they are the living image, precisely, of those loons my ancestors watched. I learn the same things from my observations of them, no doubt; experience the very interaction that my ancestors must have experienced. There is an exuberance within the live scene that cannot be felt from descriptive words or scientific books. The loons are aware of my presence, and although I cannot communicate with them in verbal terms, there's a communication nonetheless.

WHAT IS IT THAT SOFTENS our feelings and turns us against the killing of wildlife, when we know that we are predatory by nature? Is it the knowledge that we no longer need to kill for survival in most instances; therefore, we revert to benevolence, like becoming kind to an enemy who's no longer a threat? Or is it the beginnings of true reverence for life, an advancing toward a new capacity to love? "The time is coming," Albert Schweitzer wrote, ". . . when people will be amazed that it took so long for mankind to recognize that thoughtless injury to life was incompatible with ethics."

I trapped beaver throughout my early game warden years to supplement my income and to control their destruction of things deemed important by people. The argument for trapping beaver included the need to manage the population; an "overpopulation" destroys the natural habitat. Whose habitat: the beaver's, the forest's, or man's? Beaver will move their colonies once an area is depleted of adequate feed. But what about the value of shade trees they might destroy? In the lower Rio Grande Valley, where natural shade is not a commodity to be traded off, the beaver cut the cottonwood trees down along the river and drainage ditches. Shouldn't that be justification for killing some beaver? Not necessarily.

Beaver live in the lake in front of our cabin here in Alaska. They have a lodge along the shore not a hundred feet from our door, and we get pleasure from having them around. One fall, however, they decided to make use of the birch trees near the cabin while caching winter feed. They had eight or ten cut down before I realized it. My first thought was: *Those damned overgrown wharf rats will have to go.*

But there were alternatives. My oldest son and I wrapped chicken wire around the bases of the rest of the trees. You have to look closely to see the wire, and no more trees were cut. The beaver moved their operation to other parts of the lake, but still use the same lodge year after year.

I WOULD BE REMISS if I hadn't helped my children learn the basics of existing in the woods. It's difficult to imagine ever losing respect for our ancestors' abilities to overcome obstacles. If they held a reverence for life and respect for the land, they could stand tall. I don't want to think of the Alaska bush absent old woodsmen like the Tanana's Charley Smith, people who blend without disturbance into the environment; or even old Bear Moore in the upper Gila country of New Mexico, who just wanted the freedom to scratch out a bit of living from his patch of pumpkin garden, but also wanted to know there were no metes and bounds to his wanderings.

It may be true that neither one of them could write down his thoughts like John Muir or Henry David Thoreau, nor assign values in the manner of Ralph Waldo Emerson or Aldo Leopold, but that doesn't mean they couldn't feel the same pulse of the wilderness in their hearts or the same elation from a lung-full of morning mountain air. The wilderness would not be whole without them any more than it would be without the mountain lion, the grizzly bear, the Mexican gray wolf, the sight of a wild yellow columbine, the presence of a gnarled juniper snag, or the music from an exaltation of larks.

I sensed a respect for the land and its animals from many of the old-timers; the Adolph Muries, the Charley Otts, the Carl Susuis, the Deacon Deaphons. There was something they had—a knowledge, or ethic—I wasn't ready for. Could it have been simply a mellowness or wisdom that comes with age? Something suggests to me they may have always been farsighted, maybe even as children.

I don't want my grandchildren to lose the ability to survive in the out-of-doors. If they choose, they can learn the ways of the wildlife without "harvesting" them. If they choose to kill, or someday have to kill, then all I ask is that they show a respect for the wild things—taking them when they have to, but respecting them in the way the North American Indian did before the Christian European taught him a "civilized" lifestyle.

JUST NORTH of where the Arctic Circle cuts an imaginary line through the southern timbered foothills of the Brooks Range, a nondescript ridge of rock upheaval dating to the Pleistocene epoch weaves its way back into the forest. Occasionally, when I pass by this way, I am drawn to this ridge of strange rock formations.

Exploring it afoot has become something of a ritual for me; I find a peace of mind here. I have become aware of the presence of wolves on the ridge: old scat along the spine, turned white with age, consisting of small animal bones and the hair of moose, and old wolf tracks in the soft grit between patches of lichens. And sometimes I find fresh tracks in vanishing mud—fresh enough to still give off the scent of "wet dog" to a close, curious nose. It seems to me, although I know wolves cover great distances, that this place is a favorite haunt, and though I've not discovered sign of heavy use, I'm certain there's a den nearby. In the late spring, along the opposite slope from where the wolves can watch the influence of man upon the land, I might find a comfortable spot on a high southeast-facing slope, and there, out of the prevailing wind and in the warm sun, I can look east into forever, it seems, across the boreal forests of the arctic hills.